Exercises • Worksheets • Techniques • Meditations

Internal Family Systems

Skills Training Manual

Trauma-Informed Treatment for Anxiety, Depression, PTSD & Substance Abuse

Frank G. Anderson, MD • Martha Sweezy, PhD
Richard C. Schwartz, PhD

Published by
PESI Publishing & Media
PESI, Inc.
3839 White Ave
Eau Claire, WI 54703

Cover Design: Amy Rubenzer
Layout: Amy Rubenzer & Bookmasters
Editing: Marietta Whittlesey

Proudly printed in the United States of America

ISBN: 9781683730873

PESI
Publishing
& Media
www.pesipublishing.com

Dedication

I dedicate this book to my husband, my children and my parents.

First and foremost, to Michael for your ongoing and unwavering support in all my life endeavors. Your encouragement to embody and express my true self has been one of the greatest gifts of my life.

To my children Logan and Austin, by far my greatest teachers. We were brought together to learn from each other and grow together. You have changed me in ways I could never have imagined. I love you dearly and thank you for choosing me to be a mentor on your journey.

To my parents: Dad, for becoming my cheerleader and biggest fan; Mom, for telling my younger self that I could do anything I wanted to in my life. Thank you both for the sacrifices you have made and the love you have always sent my way.

With love and gratitude,

Frank Anderson

I dedicate this book to my dear friend, Pat Gercik, whose loving Self-energy puts the "P" into present, persistent, and playful.

Martha Sweezy

I dedicate this book to the late Regina Goulding, a fearless collaborator in the exploration of the traumatized inner world.

Dick Schwartz

The authors also thank Linda Jackson and Claire Zelasko for their kindness, patience, help and enthusiasm throughout this process. We also thank each other for the same.

Table of Contents

About the Authors

Frank G. Anderson, MD

Dr. Frank Anderson completed his residency in psychiatry at Harvard Medical School and specializes in understanding and treating the effects of psychic pain and trauma. He is committed to promoting compassion, hope, healing and non-violence in a troubled world.

Dr. Anderson travels around the world as a proponent and instructor of Internal Family Systems (IFS)—an evidence-based treatment that offers an accelerated path to self-awareness and healing of emotional wounds. Unique as both a psychiatrist and psychotherapist, he specializes in the treatment of trauma and dissociation in his private practice and is passionate about teaching brain-based psychotherapy, integrating current neuroscience knowledge with the IFS model of therapy. From serving as the executive director of the Foundation for Self Leadership, to conducting research and collaborating with Pixar, he also attended the Spirit of Humanity Conference in Iceland and treated survivors of the 9/11 attacks in New York City. He remains active and engaged in his profession.

Martha Sweezy, PhD

Martha Sweezy, PhD, is an assistant professor at Harvard Medical School, a program consultant and supervisor at Cambridge Health Alliance, and the former assistant director and director of training for the dialectical behavioral therapy (DBT) program at the Cambridge Health Alliance. She is the author of two articles on IFS, Treating Trauma After Dialectical Behavioral Therapy in the Journal of Psychotherapy Integration and The Teenager's Confession: Regulating Shame in Internal Family Systems Therapy in the American Journal of Psychotherapy, and co-editor/co-author of the books *Internal Family Systems Therapy: New Dimensions*, and *Innovations and Elaborations in Internal Family Systems Therapy*, as well as co-author of the book *Intimacy from the Inside Out: Courage and Compassion in Couple Therapy*. She has a therapy and consultation practice in Northampton, Massachusetts.

Richard C. Schwartz, PhD

Dr. Schwartz developed Internal Family Systems in response to clients' descriptions of experiencing various parts – many extreme – within themselves. He noticed that when these parts felt safe and had their concerns addressed, they were less disruptive and would accede to the wise leadership of what Dr. Schwartz came to call the "Self." In developing IFS, he recognized that, as in systemic family theory, parts take on characteristic roles that help define the inner world of the clients. The coordinating Self, which embodies qualities of confidence, openness, and compassion, acts as a center around which the various parts constellate. Because IFS locates the source of healing within the client, the therapist is freed to focus on guiding the client's access to his or her true Self and supporting the client in harnessing its wisdom. This approach makes IFS a non-pathologizing, hopeful framework within which to practice psychotherapy.

In 2000, he founded The Center for Self Leadership in Oak Park, Illinois. Dr. Schwartz is a featured speaker for many national psychotherapy organizations and a fellow of the American Association for Marriage and Family Therapy, and he serves on the editorial boards of four professional journals. He has published four books and over 50 articles about IFS. His books include *Internal Family Systems Therapy, Introduction to the Internal Family Systems Model*, and co-author of *Family Therapy: Concepts and Methods, The Mosaic Mind,* and *Metaframeworks*. Dr. Schwartz lisves and practices in Brookline, MA and is on the faculty of the Department of Psychiatry, Harvard School of Medicine.

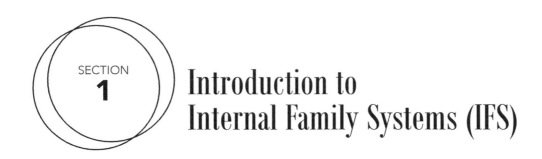

Introduction to
Internal Family Systems (IFS)

Richard C. Schwartz, who has a Ph.D. in marital and family therapy, and is one of the authors of this manual, developed internal family systems therapy (IFS) in the 1980's while treating eating disordered (ED) adolescents who routinely spoke about internal conversations with what they called "different parts." Following their vernacular lead, he referred to their subpersonalities as "parts." While exploring options and encouraging the clients to interact with their ED parts the way members of a family interact, Schwartz learned that he and the client could persuade an extreme ED part to permit the client some mental separation from its distorted perspective, whereupon the client would spontaneously become mindful (nonjudgmental and curious) toward the part.

This kindly – ultimately compassionate – relational stance between client and parts proved crucial to healing and became the linchpin of IFS therapy. We've all had moments of clarity and balance when the incessant chatter inside our head ceases, we feel calm and spacious, as if our mind, heart and soul had brightened and expanded. At other times, we feel a wave of joyful connection with others that washes away irritation, distrust, and boredom. Schwartz observed that healing just happens when therapist and client achieve a critical mass of this phenomenon, which he dubbed the *Self*.

EMBODY THE SELF AND LISTEN TO PARTS

The goal of IFS, now an evidence-based treatment, is to embody the Self and heal our injured parts so that we can live with confidence, guided by curiosity and compassion. As we illustrate throughout this manual, when clients embody more Self and listen to their parts rather than trying to eliminate these aspects of themselves, their inner dialogues change spontaneously. Their extreme voices calm down, they begin to feel good things: safer, lighter, freer, more open, more playful. Clients who've shown little insight into their problems are suddenly able to trace the trajectory of their own feelings and emotional histories with clarity and understanding. And even very disturbed clients who appear to be unlikely candidates for such shifts after living through childhoods of relentless abuse and neglect will experience insight, self-acceptance, stability and personal growth once they connect with the Self at their core.

After repeatedly witnessing a sudden acquisition of this ability to contain and understand even severe inner turmoil, Schwartz concluded that the traditional trajectory of therapy (symptom oriented, results-focused, problem solving) did not encompass, and could not help him understand, what he was tapping into. Psychotherapy and spirituality alike describe the "essence" that we call the Self with terms like soul, the divine, Buddha nature, or the core seat of our consciousness. In his experience, once parts make space we can all have access to this core of who we really are.

Yet being Self-led with clients isn't easy. So much of what we're taught about the psyche and therapy fuels our fears and keeps us distant. The DSM in all its iterations has always encouraged us to focus on our clients' scariest and most pathological behaviors, while concerns for our careers, reputations and the potential of litigation encourage us to be on guard. At the same time, since our clients stir up as many unruly feelings, thoughts, prejudices, negative associations, and untoward impulses in us as we stir up in them, our personal baggage makes us vulnerable in sessions and we cannot help our clients until we can help ourselves. We cannot go with them into their terror, humiliation and devastating loneliness unless we've explored ours first.

As a result, we can't omit and ignore our inner barbarians, those unwelcome parts who hate, rage, suppress, terrorize, betray, threaten and engage in all manner of prejudice and greed – or those who have somewhat less abhorrent feelings like depression, anxiety, self-righteousness, guilt and self-loathing. Nevertheless, once we have befriended our own extreme reactions - for befriending is a more beneficial, popular and effective activity than berating - the job of helping clients befriend theirs offers significant benefits for us therapists. When we listen to our parts rather than exiling them, we don't have to work so hard and the parts are able to transform.

To attune with our clients we must make a big investment in ourselves, which can be a challenge. But once we are able to connect internally, sessions flow with an almost effortless quality, as if something magical were unfolding. As IFS therapists, our job is to accompany our clients to a state of deep mindfulness, full-bodied attention, centered awareness, and inner calm. After a few hours in this energizing, enlivened state, having been privileged to witness the awe inspiring journeys our clients take inward, we often end the day feeling connected to something much bigger than we are.

HOW TO USE THIS BOOK

IFS is Experiential: Try Doing the Exercises in this Manual Yourself First

The best way to grasp the IFS approach to therapy is to have the experience. And the best way to practice IFS with clients is to know what it feels like personally. We recommend that readers engage with the exercises in this manual personally before using them with clients.

Meditations

This manual contains several meditations that are based on the IFS model. Feel free to use them in whatever way feels right. You may want to record them to play back, or you may be able to read them through and simply remember the steps. You may also want to go through them in sequence or you may want to try the same one several times before moving on to another.

Neuroscience

We have also incorporated some current knowledge on neuroscience as it relates to the steps of the IFS model of therapy. We hope this will enhance your understanding of what might be happening in the brain during an IFS session as well as inform your therapeutic decisions.

What a Manual on IFS Can Teach

In this manual we walk the reader through the flow of the IFS model of psychotherapy descriptively and experientially, introducing the reader to the positive motives, often hidden, that govern internal systems and illustrating effective strategies for addressing the problems that underlie symptoms.

We also illustrate the final healing steps of IFS therapy, which accompany the client into her or his greatest areas of vulnerability, but in this case we do not provide experiential exercises nor do we recommend that you try to do an unburdening. Instead we urge therapists who lack formal training in IFS to revert to their prior training and expertise at this point in therapy. To learn to practice IFS from the initial contact all the way through the final steps, and to maximize proficiency with the IFS model, we recommend the formal, experiential training offered by The Center for Self Leadership (CSL). We also recommend trying IFS therapy with an IFS therapist. For more information on the various training opportunities and a listing of IFS trained therapists, go to Selfleadership.org.

The IFS Model of Mind

IFS therapy uses a plural model of mind: we all have an internal system of countless parts who interact internally with each other and externally with other people. In addition, we all have a core resource that is not a part, which is characterized by balance, curiosity and compassion. Schwartz dubbed this non-part resource "the Self." Schwartz credits the systems focus of his family therapy training with helping him be open to conceptualizing the psyche of the individual as a system, which is consistent with what he was hearing from clients (Schwartz, 1995). In this inner system, some parts take on protective roles in response to relational injury, which is ubiquitous in childhood in one form or another and cannot be avoided. IFS attends to the needs of parts in both categories: protective and injured.

GLOSSARY OF IFS TERMS

Like all psychotherapies, IFS assigns unique meanings to certain words and phrases. Here is a glossary of the language in IFS.

5 P's: The qualities of an IFS therapist: Presence, patience, persistence, perspective, and playfulness.

6 F's: The steps we use to help protective parts differentiate from the Self. They include **F**ind, **F**ocus, **F**lesh-out, **F**eel, be**F**riend and **F**ears.

8 C's: The qualities of Self-energy: Curiosity, calm, clarity, connectedness, confidence, courage, creativity and compassion.

Blended (or **undifferentiated**): When a part is undifferentiated from another part or from the Self.

Burdened: When parts have taken on painful beliefs and feelings about themselves or have distressing physical sensations from external sources from which they cannot escape until they are unburdened.

Burdens: Negative, self-referential beliefs (*I'm unlovable, I'm worthless*) and intense, trauma-related feeling states (terror, shamefulness, rage), physical sensations or visions (flashbacks).

Direct Access: A method of communicating with parts, and an alternative to internal communication (a.k.a. in-sight). When a protector will not unblend, the therapist speaks directly to the clients' parts. In direct access the therapist can speak *explicitly* to a part (e.g., "Can I talk to that part directly? Why do you want John to drink?"). Or, when the client rejects the idea of parts, and says, "That's not a part, that's me," the therapist can speak to it *implicitly*, without direct acknowledgement that she is talking to a part. Direct access is the usual method with children (see Krause, 2013), although some children are able to use internal communication.

Do-Over: When an exiled part takes the client's Self back into a time and place in the past where it is stuck and instructs the Self to do whatever the part needed someone to do for it at the time. After this, whenever the part is ready, the Self brings the part out of that scene into the present time.

Internal communication (a.k.a. in-sight): The primary approach used with adults to understand and communicate with parts, internal communication requires that the client be aware of parts (often aided by visual, kinesthetic, or aural experience) and have enough Self-energy to communicate with them directly. When protectors block internal communication we use direct access.

Parts: Internal entities, or subpersonalities, who function independently and have a full range of feelings, thoughts, beliefs, and sensations. These entities, who have their own Self-energy when they feel understood and appreciated, vary in appearance, age, gender, talent, and interest. They exist and take on various roles within the internal system. When not exiled or in conflict with each other over how to manage exiled parts, they contribute in a variety of ways to our efficient functioning and general well-being.

Three Types of Parts

IFS classifies parts in three broad categories according to how they function in relation to each other. An injured part, or *exile*, is primary in its influence on the behavior of other parts. Orbiting around exiles are two categories of protective parts. The proactive protector, called a *manager*, has the role of maintaining the individual's functioning despite what the exiles feel. The reactive protector, called a *firefighter*, has the role of distracting from and suppressing the emotional pain of exiled parts, which breaks through despite the best efforts of the manager.

1. ***Exiles:*** Revealed in feelings, beliefs, sensations and actions, these parts have been shamed, dismissed, abused or neglected in childhood and are subsequently banished by protectors for their own safety and to keep them from overwhelming the internal system with emotional pain. A great deal of internal energy is expended to keep exiles out of awareness.

Protectors:

2. ***Proactive protectors*** or ***Managers:*** Proactive helpers who focus on learning, functioning, being prepared and stable. Managers are vigilant in trying to prevent exiles from being triggered and flooding the internal system with emotion. As a consequence, they are hard working and use a variety of tactics – not least, determined, relentless, criticizing and at times shaming – to keep us task-oriented and impervious to feelings.

3. ***Reactive protectors*** or ***Firefighters:*** Reactive protectors share the same goal as managers; they want to exile vulnerable parts and extinguish emotional pain. However, reactive protectors are emergency response workers. They get activated after the fact, when the memories and emotions of exiles break through despite the repressive efforts of managers. Reactive protectors tend to be fierce and use extreme measures that managers abhor, like alcohol and drug abuse, binge eating, excessive shopping, promiscuity, cutting, suicide and even homicide.

Polarization: An adversarial relationship between two protectors who are in conflict over how to manage an exile. Over time, their opposing views tend to become increasingly extreme and costly. However, when the intentions and contributions of each part are acknowledged by the client's Self, polarized protectors generally become willing to allow the Self to take over the job of caring for, protecting and repatriating the exile. Protectors are then freed from an onerous job and can find their preferred role in the internal family.

Post-unburdening: The three or four weeks following an unburdening are a window of time in which the physiological and emotional changes are consolidated.

Protector Check-in After Unburdening: Inviting protectors to try something new – allow the client's Self to be with (that is, heal) and protect the exile.

Retrieval: After being witnessed in whatever way it needs, an exiled part leaves the past (where it has continued to be, de facto, frozen in time) and comes into the present.

Self: The innate presence in each of us that brings balance and harmony along with certain nonjudgmental, transformative qualities (curiosity, caring, creativity, courage, calmness, connectedness, clarity, compassion, presence, patience, persistence, perspective, playfulness) to our internal family. While parts can blend with (overwhelm and therefore obscure) the Self, the Self nevertheless continues to exist and is accessible as soon as parts separate (that is, unblend).

Self-energy: The perspectives and feelings that the Self brings to the relationship with parts.

Self-led: When an individual has the capacity to hear, understand, and be present with parts, acknowledging and appreciating the importance of their roles in the internal family system and with other people.

The Invitation for Exiles: After unburdening, the part can invite qualities of its own choosing to fill the space formerly occupied by the burden.

The Unburdening Process: Taken as a whole, the unburdening process includes witnessing, do-over, retrieval, unburdening, inviting new qualities and protector check-in.

Unblended (or **differentiated**, or **separated**): The state of being-with, in which no part (e.g. feeling, thought, sensation, belief) is overwhelming the Self. When unblended parts remain separate, present and accessible but are not vying to dominate, we have access to Self-qualities. This state of being unblended is often experienced as internal spaciousness.

Unburdening: The painful emotions, traumatic sensations and harsh beliefs of an exiled part are ceremonially released, often using imagery that involves one of the elements (light, earth, air, water, fire).

Witnessing: The process in which a part shows and/or tells the client's Self about its experiences until it feels understood, accepted, self-accepting and loved.

SEE FOR YOURSELF:
PARADIGM SHIFT IN IFS

In the interest of anchoring the concepts of IFS, here is a preliminary illustration of assessment and diagnosis at the outset of an IFS therapy with a traumatized client.

On the phone before her first session, Serena offers some cursory details about her life and then firmly asserts that she doesn't want to spend a lot of time going over the past because her childhood was not the problem. She says she has tried talking about her childhood in therapy in the past but it didn't help. Mostly she is puzzled at the strong reaction she is having to her German boyfriend having broken up with her because he was leaving the United States.

SERENA: It's not like we were that serious. I just can't stop crying.

  THERAPIST: Have you been in therapy before?

SERENA: Yes it was boring. I swore I would never do it again.
  - *In this brief exchange the therapist learns a few important things about Serena, which she frames according to the IFS model.*
    - *Serena has a part who feels very sad but she has no idea why.*
    - *The relationship with her German boyfriend was either casual or a protective part is now minimizing its importance.*
    - *Something about therapy in the past was so unbearable that her protectors swore never to let her go back.*

When she comes in for the first session the therapist writes all this on a whiteboard so they can look at it together.

Serena's parts:

Can't stop crying   Relationship with boyfriend was not important

Puzzled about why Serena is crying   Will never go to therapy again!

> ### Introducing the Concept of Communicating With Parts

THERAPIST: You've mentioned all these feelings and thoughts. I often find that when we focus on them internally and listen to them, we can learn important things about ourselves. Are you open to trying this? See which part needs your attention first.

SERENA: Why can't I stop crying?

> ### Switching to Parts Language and Getting Permission to Proceed

THERAPIST: Good let's check on that. Ask if any of these other parts of you object to you helping the one who can't stop crying.
  - *Asking other parts for permission to proceed is always wise once you choose a target part.*

SERENA: It's kind of funny but I'm hearing someone yelling, "I don't want to be here!"

Welcoming All Parts

THERAPIST: You did have that part who swore never to go to therapy again so that makes sense. Is it okay to hear more?

- *Inviting polarized parts (parts who may disagree) to participate helps forestall any urge they might have to sabotage the therapy and also provides crucial information.*

SERENA: I guess so.

THERAPIST: How do you feel toward the part who doesn't want to be here?

SERENA: Kinda curious about it.

- *This more open-hearted attitude signals that we can proceed.*

Remember the Target Part

THERAPIST: Okay, first let's tell the one who can't stop crying that we'll come back to it.

- *As with family therapy, we are polite and inclusive of all parts.*

SERENA: Seems like the crying is connected to the one who doesn't want to be here but I don't know how.

THERAPIST: Would you like to find out how?

- *Checking to see if she remains curious and will be available to hear this information.*

SERENA: Yes.

- *Serena has successfully shifted into being curious about and observing her inner experience without a lot of fear or judgment.*

Making Connections

THERAPIST: Ask the one who doesn't want to be here to tell you more.

SERENA: It's afraid I'll be overwhelmed.

- *Serena has a protective part who fears that giving the crying part attention will encourage it to take over, which would overwhelm her with negative emotion.*

THERAPIST: Do you understand this fear?

- *Again checking to see if Serena remains available (curious enough) to hear more about the crying part, who is in distress.*

SERENA: I was in a car crash when I was five. My mother died. But I don't remember her so I never think about it.

- *Serena is now beginning to be aware of her parts rather than being dissociated or overwhelmed. This 5-year-old part was exiled after her mother's death. Protectors (other parts) keep the 5-year-old out of her consciousness.*

THERAPIST: We can help the 5-year-old not take you over.

- *The therapist begins to reassure Serena's protectors that the 5-year-old can separate so that she can be safely helped.*

After this first meeting, the therapist is aware of the following: Serena has a traumatized part: a 5-year-old whose life was upended by the random violence of her mother's death in a car crash. Protective parts have kept this 5-year-old out of mind. And the part who removed Serena from therapy years ago does not feel safe about her returning to therapy now because of the danger of the distressed 5-year-old's overwhelming her emotionally.

Although the therapist knows all this, much remains unknown: what do Serena's internal and external systems believe about her mother's death? She might have parts – or actual external people – who hold her responsible. She might have beliefs about god, punishment, safety and fate. She might have parts who feel survivor guilt (the belief, for example, that surpassing her mother in happiness or longevity would be a betrayal). Or parts who feel separation guilt (for example, the belief that growing up and leaving her father would wound him). This initial assessment is just a beginning. There is much to learn and therapy itself will be the learning process.

THE GOALS OF IFS

Each step of this therapy has a goal. At every point the therapist helps the client to help the part. **First**, clients help their protective parts differentiate. **Second**, clients befriend their protective parts and get permission to help wounded parts. **Third**, clients form a positive relationship with wounded parts, witness their experiences and help them to let go of feeling states and beliefs that are extreme and damaging so they can heal. Accomplishing this milestone liberates protective parts, makes room for healed parts to reintegrate and reinstates the Self as leader of the inner system.

Two Categories of Protective Parts: Proactive and Reactive

Proactive Parts

All protective parts are trying to exile the powerful negative feelings and beliefs of wounded parts with the aim of warding off more harm and keeping us safe. However protectors differ in that they are either proactive or reactive in response to emotional pain.

We call proactive parts "managers" because they try to manage our lives in ways that keep emotional pain out of consciousness. They often focus on motivating us to improve, work hard, be productive and be socially acceptable. At the extreme, however, these aims can devolve into tactics like perfectionism, intellectualizing, one-sided caretaking, obsessing about appearance, conflict avoidance at great personal cost and trying to control or please others.

Reactive Parts

We call reactive protectors "firefighters" because they try to distract from or stop emotional pain as fast as possible without consideration for consequences. These protectors view their actions the way we might view a life-saving medication with terrible side effects: If you need it, use it. Examples include bingeing, purging, addictions, numbing, dissociating and cutting as well as thoughts and behaviors related to suicide.

A CAVEAT ON PROACTIVE PROTECTORS

Although proactive protectors (managers) generally do seem managerial, any behavior that is used to prevent emotional pain is proactive. Consider, for example, that addiction and dissociation, which are generally reactive behaviors that serve to distract from intense negative feelings, can also be used to prevent us from having feelings at all. If a person goes from binge drinking to daily drinking, his reactive behavior has been recruited to the proactive role of preventing the feelings that drinking suppresses. If a person goes from dissociating in response to certain feelings to being numb and detached all the time, her reactive behavior has likewise been recruited to the proactive role of prevention. Extreme protectors are most likely to become proactive in this way in response to the looming threat of emotional overwhelm. Rather than trying to control or manage extreme protectors, in IFS we offer to resolve the underlying problem.

VULNERABLE PARTS: EXILED

When children feel shamed (often but not exclusively interpersonally) vulnerable young parts are particularly liable to develop overwhelmingly threatening beliefs like "I'm unlovable" and "I'm worthless." Equally, when experience is terrifying and beyond our capacity to tolerate, our most vulnerable parts feel stripped of significance. Protectors step in to keep their toxic beliefs out of consciousness and, as a result, vulnerable parts end up permanently alone, forgotten and often trapped in the past. They long for help but when they push into consciousness with negative feelings, beliefs, sensations and memories, protectors again experience them as a hazard. On the other hand, IFS therapists know that exiled parts are not their wounds. Clients come to therapy with exiles feeling miserable, but we know these parts will revert to their natural state of curiosity, creativity and playfulness once they are unburdened of trauma-derived beliefs. Their vitality and capacity for unself-conscious joy make a unique contribution to what Marsha Linehan calls "a life worth living" (1993).

DEFINING THE SELF

The Self is the core of psychic balance, the seat of consciousness and inner source of love. Everyone has a Self. Just as light can be both particle and wave, the Self can show up in the energy of certain feeling states (curiosity, calm, courage, compassion, love) or with the sense of an individual being present (Schwartz, 1995). But the Self is perhaps most simply introduced to clients as "the you who is not a part" (which we will use throughout this manual). Since parts who separate and get into relationship with the Self feel loved – and love provides an abiding counter to the sense of being unacceptable – the overarching goal of IFS is access to the Self. As a way of being, Self-energy helps us and our clients take a calm, curious, open stance toward inner experience. For some individuals this practice is spiritual in nature, for others it simply works.

ACCESSING THE SELF

Though extreme protective parts can block our access to it, the Self does not need to be cultivated or developed. Some meditation practices, most spiritual traditions, and some other models of psychotherapy feature a concept of core wisdom and balance similar to the Self, though using different language. Our goal in IFS is for both therapist and client to access Self-energy as a wave and to be in relationship with the Self as particle. As therapists, our practice is to be mindful of the needs of our reactive parts but to differentiate from them and be fully present with our clients.

Severe Trauma and The Self

In cases of severe trauma we think in terms of the "Self of the system," which is to say the therapist and client are one system that has access to Self-energy through the Self of the therapist. Clients who experience dissociative identity disorder (DID), for example, may have little or no access to the Self for months or years so the therapist must act as the Self of the therapeutic system. As inner attachments form and inner relationships are repaired, clients gain more access to their Self and the therapist can gradually move to a more supportive role. When the client has enough access to the Self and the baton passes from therapist to client, protectors (who are often young in age and are also traumatized) may need to be reassured that the therapist will not disappear.

When an Exile Meets the Self and Gets Mad

Often in trauma, when protectors first grant the client's Self access to the vulnerable part who has been exiled, it commonly responds with distrust or anger.

- "Where have you been?"
- "If you exist, why did I have to go through all that?"

When this kind of interaction occurs at the end of a session, we begin the next session by returning to the same part and same subject.

- Does this part want to say more to the client's Self about how it felt to be alone?
  - "What was it like to feel abandoned?"
  - "What is it like to wish this reunion had happened sooner?"

In response to these justified complaints of a part who feels abandoned, we take time to repair the relationship between it and the client's Self.

- "I apologize. You didn't deserve to be left alone. I'm so sorry I couldn't be here sooner. What has it been like for you?"
- "I'm here for you now. What do you need?"

ASSUMPTIONS IN IFS

1. All parts have good intentions, even those who misbehave. Therefore we begin therapy with a radical invitation: all parts are welcome.
2. Our psychic response to injury is predictable: when vulnerable parts are wounded other parts step into protective roles.
3. Protective parts behave in predictable ways, some of which look pathological.
4. A destabilized, disrupted inner system can become reintegrated and balanced once it is in relationship with the client's Self.
5. The Self is neither created nor cultivated and cannot be destroyed but is, rather, intrinsic and present from birth.
6. Every person has a Self, and the Self can be accessed for healing in every person.

SECTION
2

Assessment and Diagnosis

ASSESSMENT: PARTS VS. PATHOLOGY

Mental health assessment is typically organized around diagnosing pathology, which is designated according to lists of symptoms chosen by committees of professionals: bipolar disorder, schizophrenia, schizoaffective disorder, depression, PTSD, anxiety, OCD, eating disorder, addiction and a host of "personality" disorders (American Psychiatric Association, 2013). The IFS understanding of the psyche orients our assessment of a client's functioning and potential in a different direction. The mind is plural so we assess the activities of a plural mind. At the outset of therapy we hear the client's presenting complaint as one part, we then ask permission to talk to any other parts who are involved, we ask them to unblend (separate, differentiate), which makes room for the client's Self so we can explore how they serve her (if they are protectors) or (later in therapy) how they are burdened and what they need (if they are exiles).

FIRST, IS YOUR CLIENT SAFE?

Before we do anything, however, we want to know if the client is currently safe. If not, we attend to safety first. Traumatized individuals who seek therapy may lack the economic and social resources to be safe for any number of reasons. Physical safety (food, shelter and safety from violence) of course provides a platform for internal inquiry. This is not to say that we can't do parts work if a client is at risk of being undernourished, without shelter, without medical care or is in a dangerous relationship.

But in this circumstance we reach for appropriate resources (domestic violence expertise, a safe house, sources of food and medical care, etc.) to build external safety while establishing rapport in the internal system by noticing parts and setting the intention to help them. Here is an example of a client describing an incident of partner violence at home.

JOSIE: We got into an argument and he grabbed me by my hair and pulled me around the bedroom.

　THERAPIST: Has this ever happened before?

JOSIE: Once or twice.

　THERAPIST: What is this like for you?

JOSIE: I'm divided. My heart is jumping out of my chest and I'm afraid of how far he might go. But at the same time I feel so enraged that I keep screaming at him.

　THERAPIST: What do you say?

JOSIE: Oh "be a man" and other things that are guaranteed to enrage him. And I hit him. I know it's not smart but I don't feel like I can stop.

THERAPIST: Is alcohol a factor?

JOSIE: Probably. I don't think it's ever happened if we haven't been drinking.

THERAPIST: Okay. Can I make some suggestions?

JOSIE: Yes please.

THERAPIST: So let's talk about your safety right now, when you go home. First, is this over? Let's talk now about what usually happens between you after you get violent. Let's make a plan for your safety. And I will give you the number of the domestic violence hotline so you can run the plan by them before you go home. Then - and we may need to do this next week - I want to check in with all parts of you who are involved with this so we can find out who feels what and who thinks what. How does that sound?

JOSIE: That's good. I can feel that - like my heart is a little calmer.

☙✦❧

After this conversation the client and therapist can establish guidelines for: a) avoiding further violence, b) de-escalating, if possible, and c) putting other supports in place, like a connection with a domestic violence shelter. De-escalating may be beyond the client's reach in heated moments until she has become more Self-led, and her partner may in any case have demonstrated an unwillingness or inability to de-escalate. Our long-term goal is for her protectors to unblend so her Self can take the lead externally as well as internally, but this takes time. After addressing practical matters of safety, we help the client engage her internal system inclusively, without judging or exiling any part, including the ones who are attached to a violent partner, the ones who feel enraged about that, and parts who have varying opinions about what should be done both short and long term.

DOING THE INITIAL ASSESSMENT IN IFS

At the outset of therapy, before we know the client, we check on his access to Self-energy by being curious about his inner experience: How spacious is it? At what speed is it going? How weighty does it feel? How light or dark is it inside? How calm or agitated? For us, these states of being – when not governed entirely by biology – are secondary to inner relationships. The plural model of mind guides us to be curious about the instrumental nature of the client's inner relationships. How does he treat himself? Can he be kind to himself or is he hounded by self-criticism or constantly on the run? If so, why? How is self-criticism protective? What function does avoidance serve within his system? We trust that his symptomatic behavior will makes sense once we know him well enough to see it in the context of formative experiences.

In IFS, Assessment Never Ends

Since our overarching goal in IFS is to improve access to the Self, our emotional and intellectual compass, we start by assessing the level of Self-energy in both client and therapist and we continue to do this throughout therapy. For the therapist, assessing Self-energy means, first and foremost, being aware of our parts as they get activated in response to the client's parts. Secondly, we work with our triggered parts and encourage them to step back so they won't get in the way.

Do We Need Information about the Past?

In an initial assessment we listen to whatever story is relevant to the client's presenting problem, we are curious about history, and we assume that, at some point during therapy, her observations will track back to lessons from the past about danger and safety. Although this trek will be central to her process, we assume that we are not hearing the whole story at the outset of therapy. In addition, we don't need this information to do our job. We can help the client regardless of what she reports to us about historical events.

MEDICAL MODEL VS. MODEL OF MIND

In addition to posttraumatic stress disorder (PTSD) and dissociative identity disorder (DID), trauma survivors often receive a slew of other diagnoses including depression, anxiety, borderline personality disorder, or some kind of addiction to alcohol, drugs, exercise or food (Herman, 1997; Herman & van der Kolk, 1989). These diagnoses are listed in the *Diagnostic and Statistical Manual of Mental Disorders* or DSM (the latest version of which is the DSM-5®). The American Psychiatric Association (APA) developed the DSM to ground psychiatric treatment in science. Given their methodology – DSM diagnoses are based on lists of symptoms that are periodically chosen by committees of professionals who are picked by the American Psychiatric Association – this effort remains controversial (Greenberg, 2013; Fisher, 2014). Nevertheless, because the terms of the DSM continue to be widely used, the medical model approach continues to be a strong influence on the field of mental health.

A DIFFERENT APPROACH WITH TRAUMA

In IFS we simply see DSM diagnoses as various ways of describing the behaviors of activated parts. And rather than pathologizing symptomatic behaviors we view them as natural efforts to solve problems: to cope, stay safe and survive. Trauma diagnoses include posttraumatic stress disorder (PTSD), dissociative identity disorder (DID) (van der Kolk, 2011), both listed in the DSM, and complex trauma or developmental trauma disorder (D'Andrea et al, 2012; van der Kolk, 2005; van der Kolk, 2014), which is also widely used, including by the International Society for Traumatic Stress Studies (ISTSS).

Here is an IFS perspective on several diagnoses that are often given to traumatized individuals before (or in lieu of, or in addition to) receiving one of the more specifically trauma related diagnoses listed above.

- **Borderline personality disorder** (BPD): This diagnosis offers a portrait of the consecutive blending of exiles (desperate young parts, internally shunned, longing for rescue and redemption) and protectors, most notoriously (though not exclusively) the ones who forbid the risks of intimacy and the ones who believe that dying is the only way to end emotional pain.

- **Narcissistic personality disorder** (NPD): This diagnosis shows the efforts of a hard-working protector as it holds up a gilded self-portrait as a shield against the arrows of shaming – mostly inner shaming in response to feelings of inadequacy.

- **Depression:** Mood disorders are heritable but not all post-trauma depression is evidence of a genetically-based mood disorder. Since depression suppresses the body's emotional signals, deadening physical and emotional experiencing in a paralyzing (if excruciating) way, a protector who amplifies depression generally aims to inhibit while an exile who feels depressed is being inhibited.
  - To assess the client's situation, we ask: "Is this a part of you who feels depressed (exile) or a protective part who is using or magnifying depression for a reason?" *The only way to discover the function of any part you encounter is to ask.*

- **Anxiety:** As temperament research indicates (Kagan, 2010), our genes can also make us vulnerable to anxiety. And, as with depression, protectors can push this lever to exert influence.
  - "Is this a part (an exile) who feels anxious or a part (a protector) who has some reason to magnify anxiety?" Many protective parts are rooted in fear and carry some percentage of anxiety within them. Again, to find out we ask.
- **Obsessive-compulsive disorder:** OCD behaviors are generally geared toward managing anxiety. In the case of trauma, the preoccupation or behavioral repetition of OCD serves to distract from emotional pain.
  - As with depression and anxiety, to find out how a behavior serves or what story it can tell, we must ask.
- **Sociopathy:** Unless sociopathy is a product of brain damage, it is a protective part (Schwartz, 2016). With their telescopic focus and determination to suppress inner vulnerability, sociopathic protectors are paranoid, extreme and rejecting of both empathy and compassion as weakening. While they protect exiles who they view as unbearably impotent and tender, they are often polarized with other protectors whom they consider weak or caretaking. On this topic, Schwartz wrote:
  - "A perpetrator part can be thoroughly blended all the time, in which case the individual is likely to meet criteria for a DSM-5 diagnosis of antisocial personality disorder. When a perpetrator part stays blended all the time in this way and the client has no access to other parts, we consider it a manager rather than a firefighter." (2016, p.113)

Addictive disorders:

- **Drugs or alcohol:** The reactive protector who uses a drug or alcohol to distract from emotional pain can also settle into being a proactive protector who uses them to avoid feeling anything at all. This addict part is not a lone actor but is an actor in an inner dynamic.
  - Cykes (2016) elucidates the IFS perspective: "Rather than defining addiction as the behavior of one acting-out part, I define it as a systemic, cyclical process that is characterized by a power struggle between two teams of protective parts, each valiantly struggling to maintain a balanced inner system. One team is critical and judging, the other impulsive and compulsive. Their chronic, escalating struggle is intended to block... emotional pain." (p. 47)
- **Eating disorders:** ED's illustrate a protector polarity, with excess on one side and inhibition on the other.
  - **Bulimia** illustrates both sides of this polarity.
  - **Anorexia** illustrates inhibition in the driver's seat.
  - **Binge eating** illustrates disinhibition in the driver's seat.
  - **Over-exercising** illustrates inhibition in the driver's seat.
    Catanzaro (2016) describes the IFS lens on ED phenomena: "ED protectors always polarize into two camps: parts who push for restriction and control of the body and parts who reject this control and push for less restraint. Their tug-of-war keeps the client from being aware of the intense negative feelings and memories of exiled parts. While an individual's specific ED diagnosis depends on which parts dominate at any given time, the overall symptom picture, even if it isn't obvious from the client's physical appearance or self-report, always involves this dialectic between restraint and rebellion against restraint." (p. 51)

PRIORITIZING PROCESS OVER CONTENT IN THE FIRST STEPS

Until we reach one of the final steps described later as "the unburdening process," we prioritize process over content – we want to know about inner relationships, agendas and beliefs. This is very different from an approach that seeks to come to a conclusion about content (the client's symptoms) early on in therapy. The following three scenarios illustrate how an IFS session might unfold in response to a client wanting to talk about diagnosis.

CLIENT'S VIEW OF DIAGNOSIS

Scenario #1

SIMON: I'm wondering if I have schizophrenia.

THERAPIST: Let me be sure I understand. You have a part who wonders if I think you have schizophrenia?

SIMON: Yes. It wonders if you think that.

THERAPIST: Do any other parts want to be in on this conversation?

SIMON: I'll ask.

THERAPIST: Do you notice anyone else?

SIMON: I do have one part who doesn't want to hear all this. It's mad that I brought it up. See, I keep hearing that I'm mentally ill, which makes me want to drink.

Scenario #2

THERAPIST: Let me be sure I understand. You have a part who wonders if I think you have schizophrenia?

SIMON: Not exactly. It wants to know if you have enough evidence to say that I'm schizophrenic.

THERAPIST: Would it be willing to say more?

• *Always a good option when we're not sure what to do next.*

SIMON: It thinks if I had a diagnosis I could get better.

THERAPIST: Are there parts who disagree?

Scenario #3

THERAPIST: Let me be sure I understand. You have a part who wonders if I think you have schizophrenia?

SIMON: There's a part who wonders whether to trust you.

THERAPIST: So you have a part who wants to know if I'm trustworthy?

SIMON: Yes.

THERAPIST: Does this part have a view about your diagnosis?

SIMON: Yes.

THERAPIST: Would it be willing to share?

SIMON: If you say I have schizophrenia this part won't trust you.

✂〜◎

As these three scenarios illustrate, when we are curious about the client's view of diagnosis we are able to learn about the client's inner discussions and avoid getting inducted to one side of an overheated disagreement (what we call a "polarity").

ASSESSMENT AND DIAGNOSIS IN IFS

In IFS we welcome the client's symptoms upfront as an introduction to protective parts and we are always aware that wounded parts have been banished. To assess and diagnose we look at relationships and motives in the internal system. Regardless of the client's symptoms, we make certain assumptions about a predictable, commonly shared psychic structure in which protectors aim to hide the existence of emotionally vulnerable parts and guard them from being hurt again. Finally, despite protection that is focused on past and future injury, the Self is always available to heal old wounds and take the lead in a dangerous world.

Although we can translate our parts-based observations of the client into DSM diagnoses in order to communicate with other treaters and to bill insurance, in IFS we do not formulate the client's presenting problem in the pathologizing terms of the DSM. Rather, we explore inner relationships, inquire about motivation and ask about protector fears so we can discover how this particular client's inner system maps onto our basic template of the psyche (multiplicity consisting of parts and Self, and post-trauma coping that involves protectors and exiles).

Even as we assess the client's reasons for coming to therapy and her presenting problems, we begin to form relationships with her internal system by asserting the positive intentions of her protective parts and offering to introduce them to her Self. When appropriate, we also offer her a roadmap of our goals:

- No part of you needs to be exiled or sacrificed.
- You will have the opportunity to offer a new solution to the problems your hardworking inner system is trying to solve with these behaviors.
- If your parts take you up on this offer, their emotional pain will eventually be healed and they will feel freer.

PSYCHOLOGY AND BIOLOGY

While we assess the relationships and protective activities of the client's system, we also assume symptomatic behavior may derive from protective parts using biological vulnerabilities (temperament, genetics, somatics) to gain influence. Most mental health problems have both psychological and biological components. In IFS we are interested in teasing out the portion of the problem that is produced by motivated parts and the portion that is rooted in biology. We can only do this by interviewing parts. Since assumptions and generalizations may be (and often are) wrong, we rely on questions.

For example, one person may have a part who feels depressed in response to being relentlessly shamed (an exile) by an inner critic, another person may have a part who amplifies symptoms of depression to make him stay home and avoid taking risks (a protector), while another person's depression may be primarily biological. To find out who is doing what to whom and for what reason we must ask. In the example below, a client reports that he has long had chest pains with no discernible medical origin.

Healing Somatic Symptoms

$$\boxed{\text{Find}}$$

JAY: I don't feel anything

THERAPIST: Say more.

JAY: Well, when you, or anyone else for that matter – including my wife or my kids – ask me what I'm feeling I just don't know how to respond. I don't seem to feel things the way most people do.

THERAPIST: Do you want to explore this?
- *Asking for permission.*

JAY: Yeah.

THERAPIST: Would it be okay to close your eyes? Good. Now notice any thoughts, feelings or physical sensations that come up.
- *Starting with the body.*

JAY: Okay.
- *After a few seconds, Jay opens his eyes.*

JAY (continuing)**:** I'm aware of chest pains.

$$\boxed{\text{Focus}}$$

THERAPIST: Is it okay to focus on those to see what we can learn?
- *Asking for permission.*

JAY: I've had chest pains for years. That's nothing new. I've been to several doctors and they keep saying nothing is wrong. Once I even thought I was having a heart attack. I called an ambulance and went to the ER. Still nothing was wrong with me.
- *Jay is completely unaware of any psychological reason for this pain, which speaks to the high level of protection that somatizing often represents.*

THERAPIST: Would it be okay to go back inside and be curious about the chest pain? I believe all physical sensations hold important information for us.
- *Asking for permission again.*

$$\boxed{\text{Flesh Out}}$$

JAY: Okay I'll try.
- *After a few moments.*

JAY (continuing)**:** I saw myself as a boy. He must be 8 years old.
- *A part is beginning to show Jay about his experiences, we call this "witnessing."*

Therapist: What did you see?

JAY: The day my grandfather died.

THERAPIST: You look puzzled.

JAY: I am.

(Befriend)

THERAPIST: Are you open to seeing more?

JAY: Yes.

- *Jay closes his eyes and is quiet. Tears well up.*

JAY (continuing)**:** Grandpa was very important to me. My father left when I was 4 years old so he was my dad.

Therapist: Is the chest pain connected?

JAY: Yeah. I don't know how.

THERAPIST: Are you open to hearing more?

JAY: I'm really curious now.

THERAPIST: Send your curiosity to the chest pain and ask what it wants you to know.

JAY: This sounds strange but I'm getting that the chest pain helps me not to have feelings.

- *The chest pain is a protective part.*

(Assess Protector Fears)

THERAPIST: Ask it to say more about why it's important not to have feelings.

JAY: I'm seeing this fort I made in my bedroom. It was a blanket cave under a couple of chairs. I used to go in there when I was upset.

THERAPIST: Does this make sense to you?

- *Checking on Jay's Self-energy toward the boy.*

JAY: Totally.

THERAPIST: Let him know that you're getting the connection.

(Witness the Exile's Experience)

JAY: I grew up in a family that was not into feelings. When grandpa died, my mother had a birthday party for my older brother the next day. She baked a cake, wrapped the presents and set the table. Her attitude was: the show goes on.

- *Jay is now noticing the extremity of the boy's experience and he is speaking in the first person, indicating that he sees this experience from the perspective of the boy. Even so, this is not what we call a "blended" experience because the boy feels Jay is there with him, he is confidently showing Jay's Self about his experience.*

THERAPIST: What was that like for him?

JAY: Confusing. I knew it was crazy to have a party right after grandpa died. I felt like the world had ended. My brother was miserable. I'm getting that the chest pain helped me get through that time so I did not feel those feelings. It was a big distraction.

- *The chest pain is a part. Technically, we would consider the chest pain a protective part of the boy: a subpart (parts have parts). But because the boy and Jay's Self are in synch we can effectively address the chest pain as simply a part.*

THERAPIST: How do you feel toward the chest pain now?

- *Checking on Jay's level of Self-energy for this protector.*

JAY: I appreciate what it did for me. It really likes that I am getting this.

THERAPIST: I'm wondering if the chest pain would be interested in not having to work so hard?

- *This is our invitation to try something new.*

JAY: I do sense it's exhausted.

THERAPIST: If it will let us help the boy with those feelings, we can get him out of the past.

JAY: The boy wants that.

THERAPIST: So let's ask the chest pain if it will let you help the boy.

- *We always ask protective parts for permission. If we forget, they will jump in anyway.*

> Witnessing the Exile's Experience Again

JAY: Okay. I can see him in the fort in my bedroom.

THERAPIST: How do you feel toward him?

- *Checking on Jay's Self-energy.*

JAY: I feel a lot of love for him right now.

THERAPIST: Is he receiving your love?

- *Checking on the connection between the boy and Jay's Self.*

JAY: Wow, he's looking up at me and smiling.

THERAPIST: Great. What does he want you to know?

JAY: He seems really sad.

THERAPIST: Is this level of feeling okay for you?

- *Checking on the reactivity of Jay's protectors.*

JAY: It's a bit intense.

THERAPIST: Let him know that we're here to help him with his sadness. And ask him to share it with you a little at a time so you don't get overwhelmed.

- *Negotiating exile overwhelm.*

JAY: He's okay with that.

> **THERAPIST:** Good. Just be with him and let him share what he wants you to know.
>> • *Jay sits quietly for several minutes, tears streaming down his face as he witnesses the boy's grief.*

JAY: He is so sad. He's sad about my father leaving, sad about grandpa dying and sad that Mom couldn't handle feelings.

> **THERAPIST:** Does that make sense to you?

JAY: Totally.

> **THERAPIST:** Is there anything else he wants to share?

JAY: I think that's it.
>> • *When a client uses the word "think" be aware that a thinking part may have stepped in – so we ask him to ask the part for an answer directly.*

> **THERAPIST:** Ask him.

JAY: He says that the chest pain started when grandpa died because that's when I was really alone, no father, no mother and now no grandpa.

> **THERAPIST:** Wow. What does he need from you?

JAY: Just this.
>> • *We are silent until Jay shifts in his chair.*

> **THERAPIST:** Is he ready to leave that time? He can come to the present with you or go somewhere else that's safe.

JAY: He wants to be with me.

> **THERAPIST:** Okay. Are you in the bedroom with him?

JAY: I'm picking him up.

> **THERAPIST:** Great. Bring him to the present.
>> • *This is called "retrieval." But it doesn't seem to be working because Jay is now frowning.*

> **THERAPIST** (continued)**:** What's happening?

JAY: I think some other part doesn't want me to take him.

> **THERAPIST:** Ask why.

JAY: I used to get silent a lot when I was a kid. It feels like that part.

> **THERAPIST:** Would the silent part like to come too? (Jay nods.) Great. Bring it up to the present with the boy but ask it to give you a few more moments with him. We can help it afterward.
>> • *The silent part also protects the boy. Protectors often interfere during the unburdening process because they are afraid. Since Jay has plenty of Self-energy and the boy is eager for help, the therapist promises the silent part help but is firm about asking it to wait.*

JAY: It's hesitant but willing.

> **THERAPIST:** Great. It can check in with the boy very soon.

JAY: The boy is holding on to me so tightly now.

> **THERAPIST:** Is that okay with you?
>   • *Checking on Jay's Self-energy.*

JAY: It feels great to both of us.

> **THERAPIST:** Excellent.

JAY: We're now in my daughter's bedroom in my current house. That's where he seems to want to be.

> **THERAPIST:** Okay with you? Now ask him if he has shown you everything he needs you to know about this experience.
>   • *Checking to see if witnessing can be finished.*

JAY: Yes.

> **THERAPIST:** Is he ready to let go of his burdens?
>   • *After witnessing we check to see if the exile is ready to "unburden" – or let go of – toxic beliefs and extreme feeling states.*

JAY: Yes.

> **THERAPIST:** Okay. Have him check in and around his body for all the thoughts, feelings and sensations he's ready to let go. He can do it any way he chooses.
>   • *The exiled part is invited to make all the decisions.*

JAY: He wants to burn them in a bonfire.

> **THERAPIST:** Okay. Let me know when he's done.

JAY: It's so freeing!

> **THERAPIST:** Wonderful. How's he doing?

JAY: He's happy. He wants to play.

> **THERAPIST:** Now let's check with the chest pain and the silent part and anyone else who has been protecting him. Have them take a look.

JAY: They're shocked at how happy he looks right now.

> **THERAPIST:** Do they get that he's safe with you? Good. What do they need?

JAY: Strangely the chest pain wants to do something physical like ride a bike. And the silent part wants to meditate.

> **THERAPIST:** Sounds nice. Is that okay with you? Then they should do just that. Will you take care of the boy until we meet again next week by briefly checking in with him daily?

JAY: Definitely.

As we see, the distraction of somatic symptoms has protected Jay from emotional pain for many years. Effective as it can be to substitute one kind of pain for another in the short run, handling emotional pain in this way is clearly a "young" solution. Physical pain is puzzling, alarming and exhausting and does not extinguish the background noise of emotional pain. Protector actions are usually young in this way – they start young, they are cognitively young and they continue to reference the (often severely) limiting circumstances of childhood.

THE BENEFITS OF IFS FOR THERAPISTS

If you find going to work as a therapist tiring, preoccupying and overly stirring of your own fears, inadequacies and shame, IFS – in our experience – can offer relief.

- The IFS therapist is not called on to come up with the right interpretation, think up assignments, pressure clients to face the past, or put fragmented information and personalities back together again.
- We have one road map for all: access the Self. Although we know the steps that typically help us get there, our GPS is always Self-energy. When we feel lost or stumped we return to that source, tapping into our curiosity about what might be happening in this moment and calling on creativity when sessions go off the beaten path (Krause, Rosenberg & Sweezy, 2016).
- Since we view "resistance" as crucially guiding information and we don't fight extreme protectors, the IFS approach generally evokes little negative transference ("We're glad you showed up. What do you want us to know?").
- The IFS focus on helping the client manifest Self-energy pulls more for connectedness than dependency.
- The non-pathologizing approach helps our clients access an open-hearted, curious, connected frame of mind. The greater their access to this wise co-therapist – the Self – the more continual their feeling of safety and comfort.
- We have the opportunity to be with our clients in the same open-hearted, curious and connected frame of mind.
- We become more self-aware by extending curiosity toward the parts of us who get triggered by our clients.
- As we differentiate from our parts and access the Self, our parallel process is the paramount invitation for the client's system to take risks and try something new.

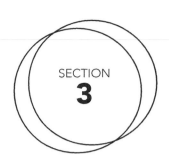

SECTION
3

Treatment and Exercises

IFS, which explicitly welcomes and deals with all symptoms (or, in the language of IFS, protective parts) from the outset, is typically an accelerated form of treatment. The open, accepting stance of IFS promotes inner safety, which invites early access to vulnerability. As protective parts begin to feel known and seen by the client's Self, which can occur within two or three sessions, they tend to relax and a client with, for instance, mild to moderate depression would experience significant relief.

In the IFS Complex Trauma Study, only one subject out of 13 still qualified for a diagnosis of PTSD after finishing 16 weeks of IFS therapy. That said, it can take weeks to months for protectors to grant the client's Self permission to be with wounded parts, depending on the severity of their injuries and the skill level of the therapist. Once granted, however, the process of the client's Self witnessing the experiences of the wounded part and helping it to unburden is usually completed within one to three sessions.

CLIENT SELECTION

IFS has been used effectively with a wide variety of mental health conditions, including but not limited to: trauma, dissociation, depression, panic, anxiety, eating disorders, addictions, OCD, ADD, bipolar disorder, personality disorders and schizophrenia. It is effective with adults, children and individuals with special needs such as autism. It has been adapted for couples therapy, group therapy, child therapy and family therapy. The main caveat involves safety: If the client's living environment is acutely dangerous or unsafe, encouraging protective parts to relax so she can connect to vulnerability (injured, exiled parts) could make her less safe. In this case we focus on safety first.

SWITCHING TO IFS TREATMENT
WITH AN ONGOING CLIENT

Most therapists come to IFS with an ongoing clientele and expertise in at least one other approach to therapy. If this is the case for you, we suggest giving some thought to which of your clients might be most open to trying something new and then introducing the model with an invitation to try it out. Such an introduction might go something like this.

THERAPIST: Remember I went to that training a couple of weeks ago to learn about this new kind of therapy? I was impressed. I thought of you and wondered if you'd like to try it.

LINA: Why did you think of me?

THERAPIST: It would be easier for me to explain that if I tell you more about the approach. Okay?

LINA: Sure.

THERAPIST: For me the cool thing about this therapy, which is called internal family systems or IFS for short, is that it focuses on how we all have many different things going on inside, which we do talk about here a lot. Like you have that part who really wanted to have a child before it was too late and then you also have an impatient part who can get so disappointed with Mickey, like when he was a colicky baby and now when he comes home from preschool acting so needy and clings to your leg. Right? And then you have a part who feels guilty about you being impatient. That part calls you a bad mother and says you should never have had a child. Right?

LINA: Yeah but we know all that. So what's different?

THERAPIST: Here's what's different, which I never knew before. Rather than talking about these parts we can actually talk to them. Want to try?

LINA: I don't know. Am I going to be your guinea pig?

THERAPIST: You're definitely going to be my guinea pig. But I wouldn't suggest it if I didn't think there was something in it for you.

LINA: If I talk to these parts and they talk back maybe they'll never shut up and that'll make my life even worse.

THERAPIST: I can understand that concern. So, although I'm just learning, this IFS training is experiential and I did it myself for a few days. I listened to my parts and I talked to them and we communicated back and forth. Like imagine if you had gone to family therapy with your parents and sisters when you were a kid. If they had all given you the opportunity to speak up, and had listened and given you the recognition you needed so much, would that have made you more or less able to listen to them?

LINA: More.

THERAPIST: Yeah. And it's the same for parts. It turns out, just like people, they want to be heard and they want their concerns to be respected. It makes them more able to take turns, not less.

LINA: So are you going to show me now?

THERAPIST: Yep. I'll show you. And, since you're the expert on you, if you like it we can learn together.

As the example illustrates, clients (and their parts) have expectations about the nature and purpose of therapy and will generally have legitimate concerns about taking a new tack. Schwartz calls IFS therapists "hope merchants" because, from the beginning to the end of a therapy, we are selling parts on the idea of trying something new. This role is particularly important if we want to persuade ongoing clients to try IFS.

STARTING IFS TREATMENT WITH A NEW CLIENT

Occasionally clients seek out a specific kind of treatment such as IFS, but more often they come to therapy because they want to feel better. At the outset of therapy some clients just want to see if the fit with this particular therapist feels good; others enter therapy with questions in hand about the therapist's theoretical orientation and style. After hearing about IFS, these latter clients may accept the idea of psychic multiplicity. On the other hand, they may be puzzled or concerned. The idea that parts are normal but some have been wounded while others are protective – and that all have good intentions – tends to be novel. When we encourage clients to "go inside," listen to their parts and connect with their Self, some will be wary while others will simply be willing. In our experience, the more we practice the more we get used to a range of responses and the more comfortable we feel responding according to the individual client's needs.

INTRODUCING KEY IFS CONCEPTS WHEN STARTING WITH A NEW CLIENT

Here is an example of how one might talk about parts and the Self when starting with a new client who wants to be oriented to your approach to therapy.

THERAPIST: Nice to meet you, Logan. Tell me why you're here and how I might help.

LOGAN: Well school has been a big drag lately. My classes are harder this semester and I feel stressed and overwhelmed. Although my girlfriend keeps trying to help me write papers, we fight all the time. It's all just super pissing me off.

THERAPIST: Sounds challenging. I'm glad you're here.

LOGAN: Yeah my parents have been harping on me to go to therapy and figure out what's wrong with me.

THERAPIST: Well, let me say upfront that I wouldn't take the view that something is wrong with you. I hear you're in a difficult place and you're trying, as best you can, to help yourself.

• *The therapist asserts a non-pathologized view of Logan's distress.*

LOGAN: Thank you! That's what I think. So what do you do?

THERAPIST: My approach to therapy is called internal family systems, or IFS.

LOGAN: My girlfriend is a psych major. What is IFS?

THERAPIST: Well, IFS is quite different. In my experience, the best introduction is direct experience - I can show you.

LOGAN: You can't tell me anything?

THERAPIST: Sure I can. This approach to therapy says that we all have lots of different parts. For example, I'm different here at work than I am at home when I play with my kids or than I am when I'm running a road race with friends. These parts are like different aspects of my personality. And I have lots more, too. Do you know what I mean?

LOGAN: I guess.

THERAPIST: Maybe it would help if I tell you what I've heard about your parts? Because in this way we're all the same. We all have parts. For example, you spoke about a part who feels overwhelmed and stressed out about school, and a part who is fighting with your girlfriend and generally seems angry all the time. As well, you mentioned having a part who disagrees with your parents that something is wrong with you. And clearly you have a part who was willing to come to therapy even though you disagree with your parents. Is that right?

LOGAN: Yes.

THERAPIST: So we all have parts and our parts take on certain roles and responsibilities to help us get through difficult times. And here's what's different about IFS. We can talk with your parts directly, if you want.

> • *The therapist leaves the decision to proceed in Logan's hands, de facto asking for permission to proceed.*

LOGAN: That sounds good. But I'm afraid if I think about all this too much I'll be more bummed out when I leave.

> • *Although one part is now intrigued, another - a concerned part - speaks up.*

THERAPIST: I understand. I don't want you to leave here feeling more bummed out. Can I tell you one more thing that might help?

LOGAN: Okay.

THERAPIST: In addition to lots of parts, we all also have internal strength to get through tough times. So deep down I'd say you do know what's best and you have the inner resources to navigate this situation. These resources include a kind of inner wisdom that is your core Self: the Logan who is not a part. I can help your parts meet that Logan if they want.

> • *The therapist introduces the idea of the Self.*

LOGAN: They don't think it's true.

THERAPIST: I'm glad they spoke up because I wouldn't want them to take my word for it. And I want them to know that meeting the Logan who is not a part would not involve them changing or giving anything up, it would just be to learn about what that Logan has to offer.

LOGAN: Okay I'll try.

THERAPIST: So let's start with one part. Who needs your attention first?

> • *Always have a target part.*

LOGAN: How about the one who's stressed out by school?

THERAPIST: Good. Turn your attention inside – you can close your eyes if you want, or not. Then notice where you find that feeling of stress in, on or around your body.

LOGAN: In my stomach. I feel kind of sick all the time.

THERAPIST: How do you feel toward that sick sensation?

LOGAN: Honestly I wish it would stop. I know I may not get A's but I'd like to get through this term without losing my mind.

- *This is another part.*

THERAPIST: So the one who wants it to stop sounds like another part who has an important perspective. But would it be willing to let you hear from the stressed part first if we ask it not to overwhelm you?

- *The therapist asks this other part for permission to proceed with the target part.*

LOGAN: Okay.

THERAPIST: Let it know that you want to help but if it takes you over, you won't be there to help. Is it willing to not overwhelm you?

LOGAN: Yes.

THERAPIST: Good. How do you feel toward the stressed part now?

- *As we illustrate throughout this manual, "how do you feel toward" is a key question for assessing how open the client is to hearing from a target part, which is the same as determining the client's level of Self-energy.*

LOGAN: Well kinda curious. I know school sucks right now, but I've been through this before. Why should it make me feel so sick and angry now?

- *Logan's answer shows that he is now open-hearted enough to listen.*

THERAPIST: How does the part respond?

LOGAN: It's shouting, *You can't fail!*

THERAPIST: Is it okay to hear more?

LOGAN: Yes.

THERAPIST: Would it be willing to speak rather than shouting?

- *The therapist begins to normalize communication between the client and his parts: no need to shout. The more Logan's Self is available, the calmer this part will be.*

LOGAN: If I listen.

THERAPIST: Are you ready to listen?

- *The therapist does not take this for granted, he is checking to see if other parts are willing to let Logan listen to the distressed part.*

LOGAN: Yes.

THERAPIST: Okay. Let it know you're listening so it doesn't need to shout. Ask it to tell you more about why you can't fail.

Logan wants a conceptual framework so the therapist introduces the basic concepts of IFS. The client, in turn, is able to feel curious about his current experience, which has been so negative and preoccupying. Not all initial sessions will cover this much territory, which is fine. Pacing in IFS is indexed to the needs, willingness and permission of protective parts: we go as fast as they let us go.

Winning Buy-in with a New Client who Isn't Interested in The Theory Of IFS

Here is an example of starting with a new client who does not ask to be oriented to the therapist's approach to therapy. He is in significant emotional pain but, because he believed he should be able to "figure this out" by himself, had been avoiding therapy.

THERAPIST: Welcome, Rory. On the phone you explained that you and your girlfriend have not been getting along, that the two of you have a 3-year-old daughter, and that they have gone to stay with her mother out in Washington State for an indefinite period of time. You also said you've been having trouble sleeping, which interferes with your ability to focus at work. Which of these concerns needs your attention first?

RORY: I really thought I could - I should be able to - handle all this myself. I didn't want to see a therapist.

THERAPIST: Should we pay attention to that?

RORY: I guess so.

THERAPIST: So let me see if I have this right, one part of you thought you should be able to handle these problems on your own but another part urged you to get help?

RORY: Yes.

THERAPIST: Which part needs your attention first?

RORY: The part that thinks I should do it on my own is really strong right now.

THERAPIST: Where do you notice that in, on or around your body?

RORY: In my head.

THERAPIST: How do you feel toward it?

RORY: I agree.

THERAPIST: So it sounds like right at this moment you're seeing things through the eyes of the part who thinks you should be able to handle all this alone. But we also know you have that other part - the one who thinks it's okay for you to get help. Where is it right now?

RORY: Out here.

• *Rory waves his hand behind his head.*

THERAPIST: I see. That one's in orbit. Would the one who's in your head be willing to make room for you inside?

RORY: Yes.

THERAPIST: So there's a Rory in there who has some wisdom and can be really helpful. With your permission, I'd like to introduce you to him. Is that okay? Good. Now ask the part who says you should do this alone to relax for a moment and don't think, just listen ... What do you hear?

RORY: I know I'm always supposed to be strong and independent, but it's okay for me to be here. I need to be a good father. This is important and I have to talk about it.

THERAPIST: Is that the part who brought you here?

RORY: I think so.

THERAPIST: Ask.

RORY: Yes.

THERAPIST: Is it still out there?

RORY: It's closer now.

THERAPIST: Would it be willing to let you talk first to the one who objects to you being here?

RORY: Okay.

THERAPIST: So how do you feel now toward the one who thinks you should do it alone?

RORY: Crowded.

THERAPIST: Would it make room for you?

RORY: How would I know?

THERAPIST: Just ask.

RORY: I don't hear anything but I do feel a bit more room inside.

THERAPIST: Great. Thank it. How do you feel toward it now?

RORY: I know where this came from. My dad thinks people who need help are weak.

THERAPIST: Let this part know what you know about that and ask if you've got it right.

RORY: Yes.

THERAPIST: What does it need from you?

RORY: It wants me to take care of this mess with Susan and be a good dad.

THERAPIST: Does that make sense to you?

RORY: That's what I'm here for.

☙

Rory came to therapy because he was losing his relationship and his child, but not all of his parts were on board with this decision. The therapist helped him notice their inner disagreement and get into relationship with them without going into the theory of IFS. Some clients ask to know more while others just get engaged and slip into the practice of relating to parts without thinking about it.

THE ROLE OF LANGUAGE

If a client objects to using the word "part" we can easily denote parts by using whatever words the client uses: I'm angry, I freak out, I'm afraid, I feel totally bummed, etc. The key to IFS therapy is our confidence in the model, hence we emphasize the therapist getting firsthand, personal experience in IFS trainings and IFS therapy. As a general piece of advice, beginners will want to start with clients who are reasonably stable and who might be interested in the model.

OUTING PROTECTORS

And one last caveat on language: sometimes a part shows up who is less than thrilled to be "outed" in therapy. We are careful to respect these parts by asking if they are willing to talk. Here is an example:

CLIENT'S PART: I'm not a part. Marc doesn't have parts.

THERAPIST: Okay. If he did have parts would that be a problem?

CLIENT'S PART: It would be if he had them.

THERAPIST: Is it okay to ask what the problem would be?

CLIENT'S PART: First of all, it's sick. And, second, no one told me.

THERAPIST: I see! That's true. I apologize. I didn't mean to startle you. You're right that no one asked you if it would be okay to talk about parts. I should have asked, but before I do, I want you to know that I don't consider having parts an illness. From my perspective we all have lots of parts and that's a good thing. So now, if it's okay with you, I'll ask. Can we talk about this?

  • *Here the therapist moves into speaking directly with the part who is in the driver's seat inside of Marc.*

CLIENT'S PART: You can say more.

THERAPIST: Well in my experience I have parts and so does everyone else. So if Marc had parts he would be totally within the norm. But whether or not we talk about parts is up to you and him.

  • *The therapist speaks directly to this protective part (referring to Marc in the third person) to reassure it that she is not trying to pathologize Marc.*

෧๙

As we see with this interaction, as well as guiding the client to speak to parts, we can always speak to parts directly as needed, a technique called Direct Access.

A TRAUMA-INFORMED THERAPY

Unlike most trauma-informed therapies, IFS is not divided into phases that focus on affect regulation and interpersonal skills that come before reviewing and integrating trauma memories. Instead "IFS starts from the premise that psychic parts constitute a motivated and purposeful inner community that does not need to be managed. We offer this community our interest and curiosity; in return the parts explain why they believe their behavior, which can seem consistently irrational and destructive to the observer, benefits the client." (Anderson & Sweezy, 2016)

Nevertheless, we do have methodology and goals: to help protectors, help the exile and harmonize all in the internal system with Self-leadership. If we think of an exile and the protectors who surround it as constituting a discrete mental beehive (of which there are many) we see that protectors, who have tremendous willingness to self-sacrifice for safety and the greater good, are very much the worker bees of the psyche while the exile is their captive queen. In IFS we help these psychic beehives one at a time and our first steps (described below as "the 6Fs") involve befriending the worker bees.

PROTECTORS SET THE PACE

IFS treatment begins by going through the 6F steps (p. 38) with protective parts, after which we move on to the "healing steps" of witnessing and unburdening exiles. To earn the trust of the inner system we often need to roll repeatedly through the steps described below, sometimes for weeks or months before protective parts give us permission to communicate with an exile directly. The more traumatized the system, the longer this may take.

GET TO KNOW YOUR SYSTEM FIRST

Before settling in with a target part for the first time, we recommend saying hello to your whole internal system. Here are two exercises and one meditation to introduce you to your parts.

- The first involves welcoming all parts.
- The second aims to help access Self-energy with protectors who have become unpopular in the system.
- The third is a meditation practice for going inside, noticing and being available to your parts. Each person experiences their parts differently, usually through one of the senses. Parts can show us a thought, feeling or sensation. Some people hear their parts, some see their parts, while others feel their parts emotionally or physically.

ALL PARTS ARE WELCOME

The simplicity of the IFS credo "all parts are welcome" can belie the courage and Self-energy required to welcome all parts. As Schwartz wrote in 2013:

> The Self-led therapist is implicitly issuing an invitation to the client: "All parts are welcome!" And from the darkest corners of their psyches come the hidden aspects of clients in all their crazy glory. And that's a good thing. The inescapable reality of therapy is that if we do our job well some clients will do all kinds of provocative things… They'll resist, get angry and critical, become hugely dependent, talk incessantly, behave dangerously between sessions, show intense vulnerability, idealize us, attack themselves, and display astounding narcissism and self-centeredness (Schwartz, 2013, p.11).

The ability to regain compassionate presence in the face of a client's extreme protectors or exiles is the *sine qua non* of a good IFS therapist. Protectors do not need us to point that out that their attempts at warding off pain are always costly failures. They know it. Instead of dwelling on the effects of their job, we ask about their goals. What do they want for the client? And we appreciate their positive intentions as well as all their hard work.

ALL PARTS
ARE WELCOME

DIRECTIONS: In IFS our credo is: All parts are welcome! Here is an exercise to help you welcome all of your parts.

Turn your attention inside and begin with this offer:

"I want to help anyone who needs help. To do that, I need to know all of you."

Then provide this information:

"If you overwhelm me, I can't be there to help you."

And make this request:

"Please be here with me rather than taking me over and, when you're ready, let me know who you are. I will write this down."

Write down the parts (thoughts, feelings or sensations) that you hear, see or sense inside (use extra paper if needed):

_____

_____

_____

_____

_____

_____

Exercise

GETTING TO KNOW
UNPOPULAR PARTS

DIRECTIONS: When we choose a target part, we need de facto permission from all other parts in order to communicate with it. To find out who might object, we ask the client "How do you feel toward this part?" As we locate reactive parts we try to persuade them to separate (that is, unblend) and let us proceed with the target part. Some target parts are particularly extreme and unpopular and will evoke a big reaction. This is an exercise for getting to know unpopular parts.

Find a target part, write it down (use extra paper to draw it if you wish):

_____

Notice how you feel toward this part and make a list of every feeling:

_____

_____

_____

_____

_____

If you are doing this alone, embody each reactive part, allowing it to do (that is, direct your posture and your movements) and say what it wishes by way of introduction.

THEN ASK IT: "Why do you feel this way toward" (the target part)?

_____

ONCE YOU UNDERSTAND, ASK: "Will you trust me to get to know (the target part) so I can help with this problem?"_____

IF THE ANSWER IS NO, ASK: "Are you willing to let me get to know you better?"

_____

IF THE ANSWER IS YES, thank the part and move on to the next until you have permission from all of them.

RETURN TO THE TARGET PART AND ASK:

- "Did you watch me negotiate with those parts who react so strongly to you?"

- "What was that like for you?"

- "What do you want me – and those parts – to know about your job and how you are trying to help?"

- "What would happen if you stopped doing this job?"

- "If we could help that part would you need to keep doing this?"

Finally, set an intention to return and help with the underlying problem (the part) this protector has named.

Meditation

GOING INSIDE TO
IDENTIFY PARTS

DIRECTIONS: Follow the prompts, and adjust as needed. You may want to write down or record what your notice.

- Settle into a comfortable position.

- Notice your back against the chair, your feet on the floor and your contact with the ground.

- Close your eyes and take a couple deep breaths if that feels comfortable. Notice.

- Focus your attention inside and notice any thoughts, feelings or sensations that show up.

    - You may notice physical sensations – some may be pleasant, others may be unpleasant.

    - You may notice one feeling or many feelings.

    - You may hear one thought or many thoughts competing with each other.

    - You may notice blankness or fogginess inside. That's okay.

- You may also notice your mind wanting to distract you and shift your focus away from that sensation, feeling or thought.

- Be curious about whatever you notice.

    - What does it want you to know?
    - What is it holding for you?

- If you can, send it gratitude for showing up, even if what you have noticed is negative.

- Notice how the part responds to your gratitude.

- When you feel ready, come back to the room.

Notice how your energy shifts when you focus your attention internally for a few minutes. Are you calmer, more peaceful or perhaps more agitated?

THE 6FS: THE STEPS WE USE TO HELP PROTECTIVE PARTS DIFFERENTIATE FROM THE SELF

The first three steps (find, focus, flesh out) involve helping parts to unblend.

1) **FIND** the part in, on or around the body.

- Who needs your attention right now?   • Where do you notice it?

2) **FOCUS** on it.

- Turn your attention inside.

3) **FLESH** it out.

- Can you see it?
  - If so, how does it look?
- If not, how do you experience it?
  - What is that like?
- How close are you to it?

4) How do you **FEEL** toward the part?

- This question is our Geiger Counter for Self-energy. Any answer that is not in the ballpark of the 8 C's means that a second part is influencing our thoughts.
  - We ask this second part if it is willing to relax so we can talk to the target part.
  - "If it is not willing to relax," we ask it what it needs us to know.
  - This process may lead us to a second (or third, fourth…) target part.
- Reactive parts often need to feel heard and validated. We stay with them until they are willing to let us get to know the target part.
- Once they agree, we ask the client, "How do you feel toward the (target) part now?"

5) Be**FRIEND** the part by finding out more about it.

- The fifth step involves learning about the target part and developing a friendly relationship. This builds relationships internally (Self to part) and externally (part to therapist).
  - "How did it get this job?"
  - "How effective is the job?"
  - "If it didn't have to do this job, what would it rather do?"
  - "How old is it?"
  - "How old does it think you are?"
  - "What else does it want you to know?"

6) What does this part **FEAR**?

- "What does it want for you?"
- "What would happen if it stopped doing this job?"

This key question will reveal any lurking polarization.
"If I stop feeling anxious, I'm afraid the suicidal part will take over." Or it will reveal the exile it protects.
"If I stop feeling anxious I'm afraid Jane will feel all alone and worthless."

TO GET TO KNOW YOUR CLIENT'S PROTECTORS: USE EITHER INTERNAL COMMUNICATION OR DIRECT ACCESS

Our goal in this manual is to facilitate your ability to spot and talk with protective parts. In the next two sections we illustrate how to combine the 6F steps with the two main strategies we have for communicating with parts: "internal communication" (that is, communication between the client's Self and the client's parts, a.k.a. in-sight) and "direct access," an essential method for those times when protectors do not feel safe enough to separate and allow internal communication. We try internal communication first because it brings the client's Self in faster. But when internal communication is not possible because the client has no access to the Self internally, we use direct access instead. In both sections we offer annotated case examples, exercises for you to practice personally and with clients, and relevant neuroscience.

INTERNAL COMMUNICATION VS. DIRECT ACCESS

INTERNAL COMMUNICATION (a.k.a. in-sight)	DIRECT ACCESS	A PROBLEM
Client's parts	Client's parts	Client's parts
Client's Self		
Therapist's Self	Therapist's Self	Therapist's parts

Later in the manual we illustrate the "unburdening process," which involves a series of steps that the client's Self goes through with exiles. However if an exiled part arises at any point while you are looking for or talking with protectors, we strongly discourage you from trying to use IFS. Missteps with protectors can be repaired with a combination of genuine concern, interest in what happened and a willingness to apologize. Missteps with exiles, however, set the protective system on high alert and may cost the client much in time, energy and suffering. If you come upon vulnerable, wounded parts we urge you to proceed with your normal therapeutic approach until you have more formal training in the IFS model (see Self-Leadership.org for training opportunities).

DECONSTRUCTING THE 6Fs

Unblending in the First 3 Steps

In IFS we aim to convince protectors to unblend (separate) and allow the client's Self to access and heal vulnerable parts. The following two cases illustrate how we do this by finding a target part, focusing on it and fleshing it out – all of which encourages the part to unblend (make room for the client's Self) so that we can proceed with internal communication (the client's Self talking to the part).

HELPING A PROTECTOR UNBLEND IN 3 STEPS

Alice's parents were unhappily married, self-involved and neglectful of her. Her working parents often left her and her younger sister home alone on various military bases. When she was 4 years old a friend of her father's stopped by when the children were alone and molested her in the bathroom of her own house. In addition, her hyper-religious, verbally and physically violent maternal grandmother lived with her family off and on throughout her childhood and terrorized her. Alice's principle protectors included a harsh critic, a bulimic and a dissociative part.

(Find a Target Part)

THERAPIST: How much of your mental time and space goes to the critic?

ALICE: Oh he gets most of it. Like 70 percent. And the fog gets the rest. The part who does stuff with
        food is not in my head so much – it just eats.

> • *The client designates a gender for the critical part.*

(Focus on the Part)

THERAPIST: I'm guessing the critic has a strong influence on the fog and the part who eats.
        Do they agree?

ALICE: Yeah.

THERAPIST: Shall we talk to the critic first, then?

> • *Asking for permission.*

ALICE: He's not fun.

THERAPIST: So other parts don't like him?

> • *Acknowledging and being curious about internal relationships.*

ALICE: They're scared of him.

THERAPIST: That makes sense. Would they let you talk to him?

> • *Asserting that the client has a Self (you).*

ALICE: Okay.

(Flesh the Part Out)

THERAPIST: Where do you notice the critic?

ALICE: In my throat.

> • *Alice's critic, a manager, lives in her throat. The fog and binging parts distract her from its
> shaming criticisms. They are firefighters.*

❧

Here is another example of Finding, Focusing On and Fleshing Out a protective part.

(Find)

THERAPIST: I hear you have a part who is angry with your girlfriend and another part who is afraid of losing her.

ENZO: Yes.

THERAPIST: Who needs your attention first?

ENZO: The angry one.

(Focus)

THERAPIST: Go inside and notice where the anger is located in, on or around your body.

ENZO: In my arms and hands.

(Flesh Out)

THERAPIST: What do you notice about that?

ENZO: He's like a boxer. He's in that *I'm ready* pose with gloves right up in front of my face.

• *Enzo finds his boxer protector, a firefighter who reacts to his girlfriend's criticisms, in his arms and hands.*

As these examples illustrate, finding a part, focusing on it and fleshing it out are all steps that foster unblending, without which internal communication between the client's Self and parts is not possible.

HELPING PARTS UNBLEND: SOME EXTERNALIZING TECHNIQUES

This topic could be elaborated on in its own book so the ideas we list below are not exhaustive. Externalizing helps parts to differentiate. While many clients are able to turn their attention inward and get enough separation from parts to communicate with them, some clients, especially those with trauma histories, are at first substantially blocked by protectors and will distract or dissociate if invited to pay attention to their internal experience. For them, externalizing options can be particularly useful and can be done with any one of a great number of props – invite your imagination and creativity.

Just as we differ in our use of externalizing props, we recommend that you play with these options to see what suits you. We also ask our clients about their creative interests and skills. Dancers may like to use movement, either literal or in the mind's eye; visual artists may wish to draw, paint or sculpt with putty or clay; fabric artists may want to sew or weave, etc.

And of course therapists who draw, paint, sculpt, dance or practice other forms of mindful movement may be particularly interested in (and good at) facilitating these activities with clients (whether they have training or not) who are open to trying something new (McConnell, 2013).

Some IFS therapists will use a whiteboard, especially at the outset of therapy when the focus is on getting to know protectors. Illustrating inner relationships has several beneficial effects: as the client's complex internal world is externalized and made more tangible on the board, he notices, listens, ponders and connects. This exploration is a respectful enactment of curiosity, an open invitation to the client's system to be seen and understood. It also illustrates the ubiquity of polarities and gives the therapist an opportunity to honor the balancing efforts of both sides in a conflict while asking some all-important questions: "Who does this one protect? What would happen if it stopped protecting in this way?" These questions reveal the exile who is being protected.

When protectors are very determined to distract, sand tray toys (which can be collected from yard sales and used with or without the sand tray) can help the client engage playfully. When a part is placed into a small figure and rendered as an external presence – a small one – its exaggerated features can be fearsome, funny or sad without being scary or overwhelming. Monsters become manageable and are invited to talk, babies of any species can be coddled in the palm and jiggled on the knee.

EXTERNALIZING PARTS

Tom grew up in a low-income housing project. He was the youngest of three boys, his mother worked two jobs and his father, an alcoholic who worked for the postal service, came home only now and then. When he did, Tom's mother fought with him verbally and sometimes physically until he left again. In the rare times Tom encountered his father sober, he saw a cold, anxious man who would not touch him. In contrast, his drunken father, whom he saw most often, was funny and affectionate.

Meanwhile Tom's older siblings and other kids in the neighborhood picked on Tom because he was small for his age. When Tom came for therapy he was on disability, had been clean from heroin for four years and he dressed as if he were a member of a motorcycle gang.

Tom came to therapy because his psychiatrist asked him to. He often came late - frequently missing half the session. He felt overwhelmed by the alcohol counseling training program he was taking. And because he was struggling with urges to use, he was afraid if he went to AA or NA he would make connections to score drugs. His parts would not unblend so most sessions involved the therapist using direct access to speak to his parts. After three months he said he felt worse after sessions and wasn't sure that continuing was a good idea because the urge to use heroin just kept getting stronger.

THERAPIST: Thank you for letting me know. Can we go over all this? In sessions we talk to the part who wants you to go to a meditation center, the part who makes you sleep all day, the part who thinks you'll flunk classes and the part who eats a lot of junk food. They all think you're that lonely kid who struggles in school and gets teased by other kids. And they don't believe there's a Tom in there who has internal strength, not a part, right? Meanwhile the guy who uses heroin tells you he knows how to stop all this. That's a sure bet. He's done it before. I have a question for him. Would he be willing to try something new first? If he's willing, I want him to be the first to meet you, the Tom who's not a part.

- *Tom is silent, looking out the window for a few moments.*

TOM: Reluctantly.

- *The therapist pulls two smallish tables in front of his chair and places a tray of toy figures on the tables.*

> (Find, Focus and Flesh Out All in One)

THERAPIST: Ask the heroin-using part to pick someone from here to represent him.

- *Tom looks at the figures carefully. They run the gamut from monsters to baby animals to kids and human babies. He picks a monster figure with its big mouth wide open and its arms looming in the air to intimidate.*

TOM: This is him.

THERAPIST: Put him on that table wherever he wants to be. How do you feel toward him?

TOM: He scares me. And I like him a lot.

THERAPIST: Let both of those parts pick figures to represent them, too.

- *Tom picks out two figures: a lamb and a tall female whose limbs are sewed on. She looks like a cross between Frankenstein and a zombie.*

THERAPIST (continued)**:** Where do they want to be while you talk to him?

TOM: This one wants to be behind me.

> • *He puts the lamb out of sight behind his back on the chair.*

TOM (continued)**:** This one wants to be right next to him.

> • *Tom places the female Frankenstein zombie next to the monster.*

(Feel Toward)

THERAPIST: Now how do you feel toward the heroin guy?

TOM: Sad. He's done a lot of damage but I know he was just trying to help.

THERAPIST: How does he respond?

TOM: He's puzzled. He doesn't know who I am.

(Befriend)

THERAPIST: He might be interested to know that you can help that part he protects.

TOM: He says I've done a crappy job so far.

THERAPIST: He might be interested in this, too. When a part takes you over you can't be there to help. For you to be able to help, everyone has to agree to give you room. Would he be willing to go first? If any other parts step in, we'll ask them to make room for you, too.

TOM: He wonders what your game is.

THERAPIST: Okay. That's a fair question. Let him know we're not trying to get rid of him. My goal is for all your parts to feel better, including him. He could quit all this and do something else - whatever he wanted. Would he like that?

TOM: He might.

THERAPIST: Would he let us show him what's possible?

TOM: He'll give it a shot as long as we know he's not going anywhere.

THERAPIST: Great. Do we have his permission to ask who needs your attention first?

> • *Asking for permission.*

TOM: Yes.

❧

By finding and focusing on his vulnerable part, an exile, as well as his very wary heroin using protector, a firefighter, Tom was able to help the latter part begin to differentiate, which helped him befriend it and get its permission to proceed.

As this vignette illustrates, externalizing parts encourages them to unblend and notice the client's Self. IFS therapists often find ways to suit themselves as they get creative with externalizing strategies. Other options include colorful scarves, pillows of various shapes and sizes, stuffed animals, or paper plates on which a part's identity can be written. When it comes to externalizing parts, we have the opportunity to be creative and invent new options.

FIND, FOCUS ON AND
FLESH OUT A TARGET PART

DIRECTIONS: This exercise walks you through the process of locating a target part. You may want to record the instructions below on a phone or other device so you can listen to them. Begin by turning your attention inside.

- Breathe and go slow.
- Remind your parts that there is room for everyone.
- Notice sensations, feelings and thoughts.
    - Ask:
        "Who needs my attention?"

Write that down:

_____

_____

- Continue to observe, be patient, and notice what shows up.
- Notice if any sensations, feelings or thoughts are being dismissed internally as insignificant or not real.

If so, start by being curious about the part who is trying to steer you this way. Write that down:

_____

_____

If not, choose whatever comes to mind first as your starting point. Notice where this part (sensation, feeling, thought) is located in, on or around your body.

- Do you see the part?
- Feel it?
- Hear it?
- Sense it in some other way?

Write down what you notice:

_____

_____

_____

_____

REMEMBER THE TARGET PART FROM THE WEEK BEFORE

Whether we are at the very beginning of a therapy or we are in midstream, we go through the steps of finding, focusing on and fleshing out target parts repeatedly. However, given the arbitrary time constraints of therapy sessions, once a therapy has been launched and we are in process week-to-week, we may not finish helping a particular part in one session so we return to it the next. Failing to do this can interrupt the flow of therapy and challenge the ability of protectors to develop trust. Consistency is as important in IFS therapy as it is in the lives of children.

We set the intention to return to a part jointly with the client. Since protectors who ward off pain often cause clients to forget the content of sessions, we can invite clients to record sessions and listen to them during the week. But either way the job of remembering at the start of the next session falls to us, so we make a note. If the client continually brings up a different part each week and objects to going back to the same target part, make a case for doing so anyway. If the client still insists on changing the subject, be curious about why and let the previous part know that we will come back to it later. The parts who are involved will notice. When we are reliable we win trust.

BEING CONSISTENT ABOUT GOING BACK TO A PART FROM THE PREVIOUS WEEK

THERAPIST: Is there anything we need to touch on before we go back to the part who felt so criticized by your grandmother?

MEGAN: Oh yeah. I forgot.

- *A protector.*

THERAPIST: Remember we set the intention to come back to her?

MEGAN: Did we? I'm feeling all that is pretty distant right now. I had an argument with Billy and I just don't know if I should be dating him again. That feels much more important right now.

- *A protector wants to change the subject.*

THERAPIST: I understand why that feels important. How about we split the time and check in on the 10-year-old who we were talking to last week first.

- *Negotiating.*

MEGAN: I don't think there will be enough time for everything. I really need to think about my relationship with Billy.

- *A protector.*

THERAPIST: I can understand that. But there is a problem. If you don't follow through on promises, your parts won't trust you. So I want to make the case for doing both.

- *Validating and making the case to this protector that it's important to let us go back to the part from last week.*

MEGAN: You know I'm just hearing "It's a bad idea!"

THERAPIST: Really? Can we ask why? What would happen if this part let you talk to the 10-year-old from last week now?

- *Checking on protector fears.*

MEGAN: I'll feel overwhelmed. I have a lot to do at work this week.

THERAPIST: If the 10-year-old agrees not to overwhelm you, could we check-in with her again?

• *Addressing that fear.*

MEGAN: Okay – only if she agrees.

જ⌐૭

Megan had been talking to an exile the week before (the 10-year-old). A protector who feared Megan would be overwhelmed by the feelings of this exile had taken over during the week and was reluctant to let that line of inquiry proceed.

Since the protector was concerned about emotional overwhelm and tried to prevent her from going back to the target part from the week before, the therapist had to be polite but persistent, exploring the resistance and addressing the concern. If she had not done so, the target part would have felt abandoned.

UPDATING PROTECTORS IN THE PROCESS OF UNBLENDING

We work to reverse the parentification of young parts. These parts, who have been inducted into an enduring sense of responsibility for exiled vulnerability in adult caretakers, may not be able to conceive of a responsible adult and will often be deeply distrustful of the client (and therapist) as adults at first. We therefore emphasize our intention to reverse the formerly upended order of care. With the aim of helping protectors let go of oppressive responsibilities and return to being children we often:

1. Ask protectors how old they think the client is (the answer is often in the single digits).
2. Guide the client to correct this notion by introducing them to the client's Self.
   a. "Let the part know that you're grown up now. Can it see you? Offer to show it around your life."
3. Guide the client to repeatedly offer help and love to protectors as well as to the exiles they protect.

Overwhelming experiences that threaten the client's survival typically open a chasm between parts and the client's Self. Traumatized protectors commonly believe that the Self was rendered helpless during the trauma and is also stuck in the past. Introducing the client's "Self of today" shows the protector that the Self survived and is available to heal wounded exiles.

Updating a Part

CHARLEY: I hide food. It even seems crazy to me. My husband finds muffins and bagels in my bureau or my bedside table and he thinks it's pretty strange but he just laughs.

THERAPIST: Does that part know you have plenty of food now?

CHARLEY: My mom put a chain around the fridge and padlocked it. We were always hungry. My youngest brother and I used to go around the back of Stop & Shop at night to get the fruit and vegetables they threw out.

THERAPIST: Does the part who stashes food for you now know that things have changed?

CHARLEY: No.

THERAPIST: Ask how old it thinks you are and don't censor the answer, just say what comes up.

CHARLEY: Strangely, I hear 10 years old. That really surprises me.

THERAPIST: That's when your dad left, right?

CHARLEY: Yes. We really had nothing for a while there. But it was late summer so we kids found berries in the woods and stole from the farmer next door. When school started my mom got hospitalized and we were sent to foster homes.

THERAPIST: Let's give your food stashing part a chance to get to know the you who is not a part. Would he like a tour of your life today?

CHARLEY: He's amazed. He had no idea.

THERAPIST: What do you say to him about food?

CHARLEY: We're okay. That's never going to happen again. I'm showing him how our refrigerator opens and closes and we have a shopping list so he can pick whatever he wants.

❧

Charley's food stashing protector still saw Charley as a starving 10-year-old boy, not an adult man with a husband and refrigerator of his own that is full of food.

As we see in this example, parts can be completely unaware of the present, in which case they need to be updated.

THE FIRST 3 STEPS:
FIND, FOCUS AND FLESH OUT A PROTECTIVE PART

Find

- Ask:

    "Which part needs your attention today?"
- Or, listen to the client talk.
- Repeat (or write on a whiteboard) the major themes you hear.
- Ask:

    "Of these parts who needs your attention first?"

Focus

- Invite the client to go inside and notice where the part is located in, on or around the body.
- Invite the client to focus on that.

    - Focusing on a part internally is different from talking about it.

Flesh Out

- Ask:

    "How do you experience this part? Do you see it? Feel it? Hear it? Or is there some other way in which you are aware of it?"
- Ask:

    "How old is this part?"

    "How old does the part think you are?"

AFTER FIND, FOCUS AND FLESH OUT: A FORK IN THE ROAD

The 6F steps help us form the alliance we need with protectors. At this point, after the first three steps and before the last three, we come to a fork in the road: if the client's protectors have been willing to unblend, you will continue through the last steps using internal communication. But if you are not able to convince protectors to separate – which is often the case with trauma – you have to give up (for the moment) and move to "direct access" (the therapist's Self talking directly to the client's part). But before describing direct access in detail (starting on p. 102), we will introduce some neuroscience concepts that are relevant to IFS and finish illustrating how to work with protective parts using the technique called internal communication.

INTRODUCTION TO NEUROSCIENCE

The "decade of the brain" met the world of psychotherapy several years ago now, with leaders in the field of neuroscience emerging to help us better understand what is happening in the brain during psychotherapy and how we can effectively help people heal from the sequelae of traumatic experiences. Knowledge of neuroscience can also inform therapeutic decision-making. For example, under what circumstances does it make most sense for the therapist to remain calm and non-reactive? And when is it best to be confident and speak up? In addition, when does it make sense to slow down and work with the body? In this manual, we incorporate what we believe is happening in the brain as it relates to the IFS model of therapy.

SCIENCE: THE MIND–BRAIN RELATIONSHIP

Many mental health theorists and practitioners distinguish between mind and brain in the following way: as the mind deals with energy and the flow of information, it primarily relates to *functioning*, while the brain relates to *structure*, defined as a collection of interconnected neurons, networks and neurotransmitters in the head, both of which interact with the body and the environment (Siegel, 2017).

As therapists we deal with both: the mind when our clients notice and interact with their thoughts, feeling and sensations, and the brain when internal attention allows for therapeutic change which coincides with structural changes in the brain (neuroplasticity). Some scientists also believe that the mind is capable of changing states, rapidly moving from one cluster of mental activity (or collection of neural networks) to the next, each serving a specific function (Siegel, 2017). This view is consistent with the most basic premise of IFS: that the psyche (mind) is naturally comprised of different parts (mental states) that are capable of blending or stepping back (shifting states).

We believe that parts use both the brain and the mind, primarily living in the mind and utilizing the brain. Parts have a range of thoughts, feelings and sensations, and they use the neural networks that correspond with those specific thoughts, feelings and sensations in the brain to express themselves.

THE SCIENCE OF FIND: INDENTIFYING PARTS

Groups of nerve cells (neurons) come together to form neuronal circuits or networks. Neuroscientists are continually discovering, mapping out and identifying various brain networks, which run the gamut from the brain at rest to empathy, compassion, grief, care, seeking and panic along with those networks that have been affected by traumatic experience.

In IFS terms, the process of finding a target part involves the mind focusing energy and attention on a specific cluster of neural networks that serve a specific function.

THE SCIENCE OF FOCUS: GOING INSIDE AND MEDITATION

When we talk about focus we are generally describing how we pay attention. When we are externally engaged – focusing outside ourselves on our environment or our relationships – we are utilizing *exteroceptive awareness* (Seppala, 2012), which primarily relies on the prefrontal cortex. *Interoceptive awareness* (Seppala, 2012), on the other hand, involves internal focus and relies on deeper brain structures such as: the brainstem (linked to physical sensations like heart rate and breathing), the limbic system (emotional integration), the insula (body awareness) and the posterior cingulate (connected to self-awareness) – all of which are affected by trauma.

Talk therapy typically utilizes exteroceptive awareness, with clients focusing their attention on dialogue with the therapist. In contrast, in IFS we invite our clients to go inside and focus internally (interoceptively) on the relationship between themselves and their parts. Interoceptive awareness is said to have more power to influence our level of happiness (Seppala, 2012).

There are of course many different forms of meditation. Mindfulness, described by Kabat-Zinn as a nonjudgmental awareness of the present moment (Kabat-Zinn, 2003) is one popular form of meditation that has been studied and shown to have both physical and mental health benefits. Regarding trauma, meditation is known to have a positive effect on several brain structures that are adversely affected in people who live through overwhelming experiences. In IFS, meditation aids clients with the process of unblending from parts and accessing Self-energy. Mindful separation, or the ability to unblend and *be with* rather than *being in* an experience is a prerequisite for the final steps of healing in IFS because reexperiencing (reliving without a validating inner audience) is not therapeutic.

THE SCIENCE OF FLESH IT OUT: CLARIFYING THE PART

Once the client has identified the target part and begins to focus his attention internally we guide him to engage with the part. This generally occurs with the mind's eye but for those who are not visual the experience can be sensory, kinesthetic or aural.

- Where is the part located in or around the body?
- Does he see it? Feel it?
- Or perhaps hear it?
- Does the part have a shape?
- A color?
- A size?
- A sound?
- How old is it?
- How close is he to it?

All of these questions help the therapist and the client to flesh out and better identify the part.

In IFS many protective parts (otherwise known as symptoms) are rooted in fear. They tend to overwork and cause upset. We believe these parts live in the mind and express themselves by connecting with unintegrated (or dysregulated) neural circuits in the brain, which typically over- or under-function and result in psychic pain. Once the wounded (exiled) part is healed, protective parts are able to let go of their job, function normally (as they did before the wounding occurred) and structurally integrate back into the larger system.

GET TO KNOW A PART

This meditation is designed to help you get to know a little bit about a part that you want to help or change your relationship with.

- *If it feels good, go ahead and take a deep breath.*

- *And think of a part who you'd like get to know a little better.*

- *Go ahead and focus on that part wherever you find it, in, on or around your body.*
  — *If you can't focus on it, that's okay.*

- *Either way, notice how you feel toward it.*

- *If you feel anything other than curiosity or acceptance, ask the reactive part if it would be willing to separate from you and not interfere just so you can learn more about your target part. We're not going to let it take over, we're just going to get to know it.*

- *And keep doing that with reactive parts until you feel curious about the original part.*

- *You may find that you don't get there, that other parts won't separate, which is okay. You can just spend the time listening to their fears about separating.*

- *But if they do let you feel at least curious about the original one then it's safe to listen.*

- *What does that original part want you to know about itself?*

- *What has the part been trying to do for you? To you?*

- *What might it need from you?*

I'll stop talking for a little while now and let you get to know it and then come back with time to return.

- *Okay, in the next few minutes we'll begin to come back.*

- *Thank the part for letting you know about it.*

- *And let it know this doesn't have to be its only chance to talk to you. If it wants, you can come back to it another time.*

- *And before you come back to this room, make sure you thank all the other parts for letting you get to know this one or letting you know that they were afraid if they didn't.*

- *And when all that feels complete, you can, if it feels right, begin to take some deep breaths again and shift your focus back to the outside.*

THE 4TH STEP: ASSESSING SELF-ENERGY WITH FEEL TOWARD

Our overall goal is for all parts – the target part and any reactive secondary parts – to differentiate and make room for the client's Self to heal the wounded part. The 4th step contributes to this goal by helping us check on the client's level of access to the Self. The question "How do you feel toward this (the target) part?" is our Geiger Counter for Self-energy (and, conversely, for blended parts).

As we assess the client's inner relational milieu in this way we may hear that someone is scared of the target part, that someone is afraid the target part will overwhelm or it's so crowded inside that there is no room for the Self. By checking on the internal scene in this way, we locate any parts who need reassurance.

Here are two examples of using the 4th step—along with two exercises for accessing Self-energy.

4TH STEP: FEEL TOWARD

(Feel Toward)

THERAPIST: How do you feel toward the boxer part?

ENZO: He protects me! I like that.

> **THERAPIST:** How does he respond?
> - *The protector's response will tell the therapist whether Enzo's appreciation is from the Self or another part.*

ENZO: He's used to ignoring me.

> - *Enzo's appreciation is from a part – the boxer would not be ignoring the client's Self.*

> **THERAPIST:** Because?

ENZO: He thinks I'm weak.

(Flesh Out)

> **THERAPIST:** How old does he think you are?

ENZO: Oh… a little kid.

> **THERAPIST:** So the little kid appreciates the boxer? And the boxer thinks the little kid is weak. Would the little kid be willing to separate so you can talk to the boxer?
> - *We ask secondary parts – in this case the little kid – to differentiate so the client's Self can be present and talk to the target part. Our goal is to get the client's Self in the middle between this protector and this exile.*

ENZO: He says okay.

(Feel Toward)

> **THERAPIST:** How do you feel toward the boxer now?
> - *Assessing the client's Self-energy again.*

ENZO: He turned around to look at me for the first time. He's surprised. He doesn't know me. I'm thanking him for all his help.

> - *When the little kid separates, the protector notices the client's Self.*

◦✒◦

In this example we see two parts, a protector and the exile it protects, becoming aware of the client's Self for the first time simply because the therapist's Self is guiding them and holding the space for this to happen.

Exercise

FEEL TOWARD

_____

DIRECTIONS: Locate a target part, focus on and flesh it out, and then ask:

"How do I feel toward _____ [the target part]?"

Write the answer down:

_____

_____

If the answer is one of the feelings (or some simile) in the list below that indicates Self-energy, move on to befriending the part.

**FEELINGS THAT INDICATE THE CLIENT
HAS SELF-ENERGY FOR THE TARGET PART:**

- Curious
- Open
- Kindly
- Caring
- Connected
- Concerned
- Compassionate
- Loving

If, however, the answer is "I understand," you need to notice whether you are hearing from a manager who forestalls feelings by staying in thoughts and telling a story that sounds plausible; or if you really have a heartfelt connection with the part and you are aware how it feels.

If you are not sure where this "I understand" comes from, tell the target part what you understand and ask if you've got it right.

If, on the other hand, you hear "I agree with this part" then the part is not yet differentiated enough from you to have a conversation. Ask it to separate so you can talk.

And if the answer is any other feeling (for example, hatred, anger, fear, embarrassment) ask the part who feels that way: "What are you concerned would happen if you were to relax and let me talk to _____(the target part)?"

Reactive parts commonly fear the target part in some way. Write down whatever you hear:

_____

_____

_____

If the reactive part fears the target part gaining too much influence, ask:

"If _____(the target part) would agree not to take over, would you let me talk to it?"

If the reactive part replies:

"That will never work," you can reassure it in two ways, first by asking, "Can we hear from _____ (the target part) directly about whether it's willing to not take over?" And then by saying to the reactive part: "You're the boss. I'm not trying to make you do anything you're not comfortable with. But if you let me hear from both sides, I can help with this conflict between you and _____ (the target part.)"

Assessing the Client's Level of Self-energy in the 4th Step

> Feeling Toward

Polly has noticed a critical part, and described it as a little man in a business suit.

THERAPIST: How do you feel toward this critic?

> • *In response to this question we listen for the reactivity of other parts in her answer.*

POLLY: I don't like him.

THERAPIST: Would that part be willing to let you handle this?

> • *Asking permission again.*

POLLY: I doubt it.

> • *The reactive part is not inclined to cooperate and let the client talk to the target part (the little man in the business suit). This tells the therapist that the reactive part believes the target part is a hazard.*

> Fleshing Out

THERAPIST: So you have a part who dislikes the critic and doesn't trust him. Can I ask a question? Who does this distrustful part think you are?

> • *The client's answer to this question will reveal the vulnerable part.*

POLLY: A kid.

> Enough Self-Energy?

THERAPIST: What do you say to it?

> • *Assessing how blended the vulnerable part is with Polly - if it is blended then Polly will say she does feel like a kid.*

POLLY: I'm not a kid. I'd actually like to talk to the critic. I do sometimes wonder why he goes on and on like that.

> • *Polly's Self is present.*

THERAPIST: See if everyone inside will let you ask the critic why he goes on and on like this.

> • *Asking all worried parts to relax and let Polly's Self talk with the critic.*

❧

In this example, we discover Polly's Self is present simply by noting how Polly responds to the protector who believes she is still a child.

Exercise

ASSESS SELF-ENERGY:
FEEL TOWARD

DIRECTIONS: For the sake of clarity, the target part in this exercise will be a chronically anxious part – but you can write in the part you hear about internally.

ASK: "How do you feel toward the _____ [anxious] part?"

- If the client is significantly differentiated from reactive parts and says something along the lines of "I'm curious" or "I care" then proceed and be curious: "What does this part want to tell you about itself?"
- But if the client has a negative reaction like "I hate it!"
- Or, the client expresses agreement along the lines "Of course I feel anxious."

ASK: "Does this _____ (hating or agreeing) part need your attention first or would it be willing to relax and let you be curious about the _____ [anxious] part?"

- If the reactive part is willing to relax, repeat the original question: "How do you feel toward the_____ [anxious] part now?"
- If, however, the client goes on agreeing with the anxious part, we guide the client to inquire whether the anxious part is blended.

  To do this, simply ask: "Is the _____ (anxious) part blended with you right now?"

    - If yes: "Would it be willing to separate and meet you?" (meaning the client's Self)
    - If no then we explore more to find out who is agreeing: "Okay, somebody else agrees and maybe that part wants to say something. Let's ask all the parts who agree on this issue to meet with you in a group. Would they be willing to do that? Invite them all to join you at a big conference table and see who shows up."

After choosing a target part, the goal is to persuade reactive parts to unblend (differentiate), which will allow the client's Self to be present and befriend the target part. When a part reacts negatively (or positively) to the target part and will not unblend, we move on to the method called "direct access."

A CAVEAT: BE AWARE OF SELF-LIKE PARTS IN THE 4TH STEP (FEEL TOWARD)

Self-like parts present with expressions of feeling that sound like the Self ("I care, I want to help") and they often stand in for the Self in the mind's eye, but they are protective parts, which means they are not equipped to heal wounds. An exiled part may feel very attached to a Self-like part who has been comforting it over the years or it may feel smothered and resentful. In either case, when we mistake a Self-like part and proceed as if it is the Self, progress often moves too quickly and easily, or halts altogether and the exile can seem perversely uncooperative. This is a sign that a Self-like part is at work and needs help to relax and trust the client's Self. Self-like parts can also show up when the client's parts are trying to please the therapist and are overly compliant. Self-like parts are common in trauma survivors because sensing the needs of others and giving them what they want can be protective.

SPOTTING A SELF-LIKE PART:
WHEN PROGRESS IS TOO FAST AND EASY

(Find)

THERAPIST: Would your depressed part be willing to separate so you can get to know it better?

BRENT: Yes, it will.

THERAPIST: How do you feel toward it now?

BRENT: I feel fine about it.

THERAPIST: Would the part who feels fine also step back?

BRENT: Sure.

THERAPIST: How do you feel toward the depressed part now?

BRENT: I feel compassionate.

THERAPIST: Is it taking that in?

BRENT: Sure.

- *Brent seems disconnected. The therapist senses he has no traction internally.*

(Find and Focus)

THERAPIST: I'm wondering if you have a part who is trying to help move things along?

BRENT: What do you mean?

THERAPIST: Is someone trying to help? Take a moment to ask inside.

BRENT: Actually there is. How did you know? There's a part who wants to help you and me so it says what it thinks you want to hear.

THERAPIST: Thank it. And ask if it would be willing take a break and watch us. We'll be okay whatever comes up, even hard things.

- *Asking for permission.*

BRENT: I'll ask.

> • *He closes his eyes and is silent for several seconds.*

BRENT (continuing)**:** I think this part is around a lot. It wants to do the right thing. It's been with me a long time.

$$\boxed{\text{Feel Toward}}$$

THERAPIST: I bet it's been helpful. How do you feel toward it?

BRENT: I appreciate it.

$$\boxed{\text{Befriend}}$$

THERAPIST: Let it know.

BRENT: It likes that.

THERAPIST: Is it willing to trust you?

> • *Will this part unblend? Is it willing to notice the client's Self?*

BRENT: It's not so sure about that.

THERAPIST: How old does it think you are?

BRENT: Fifteen.

THERAPIST: What do you say to that?

> • *Inviting the client's Self to take the lead.*

BRENT: The 15-year-old is depressed. This part is confused and thinks I'm him.

> • *The Self is present.*

THERAPIST: Does it see you now?

> • *Still befriending.*

BRENT: Yeah. It's kinda shocked.

THERAPIST: Would it let you help the 15-year-old?

> • *Asking for permission.*

BRENT: It's confused by all this. It's always taken care of me.

> • *Brent is describing a protective part in the Self-like role – that is, this protector stands in for Brent's Self and tries to handle his life and take care of younger parts.*

$$\boxed{\text{Flesh Out}}$$

THERAPIST: It stands in for you?

BRENT: It sorta *is* me.

> • *Self-like parts often insist: I am the client.*

THERAPIST: I hear it has taken the lead because it had to and wasn't aware of the Brent who's not a part. What's it like for this hard working part to meet you?

- *Asserting that the client has a Self.*

(Protector Fears)

BRENT: It's really surprised. What will happen to it?

THERAPIST: It won't go away. It will still be part of you.

- *Reassuring the protector.*

BRENT: That's a relief.

THERAPIST: It's worked so hard. Will it accept your help?

BRENT: It's thinking. It is tired.

- *Self-like parts often need a lot of reassurance before they are willing to turn the keys over to the Self. Don't worry – be persistent.*

∾

If you feel a puzzling lack of traction in a session or things move too easily, suspect a Self-like part. As this example illustrates, one of the ways Self-like parts manifest is by making the client seem "cooperative" when he is essentially absent.

SCIENCE: ACCESSING THE SELF WITH FEEL TOWARD

Neuroscience is exploring brain structures that correlate with self-definition, including how we represent, evaluate and monitor ourselves. These activities are connected, respectively, to the medial prefrontal cortex, the dorsal lateral prefrontal cortex and the anterior cingulate (Nortoff & Bermpohl, 2004). We know that self-identity also involves connections to our body and physical sensations through a structure called the insula (Lanius, 2010). Although these advances in neuroscience help us understand how the brain is involved in contextual self-awareness they are different from the IFS concept of the Self.

The Self of IFS, involving a state of calm, curiosity, confidence, courageousness, clarity, connectedness, compassion and creativity, is not, in our view, located in any specific brain structure. We believe that the Self, which is *a state of being*, is located within the mind just like protective parts – but there is a difference. Protectors who developed in response to either small or capital T trauma and show up as symptoms use unintegrated networks in the brain. In contrast, **the Self accesses *integrated* neural networks and connects to the external world spontaneously. From our perspective, the experience of "being in Self" (as we say in IFS) is internally and externally connected and maximally integrative.** In short, the Self possesses inherent wisdom and the capacity for healing. In our view, once liberated from extreme roles protectors revert to using integrated neural networks as well.

SCIENCE: THE NEUROBIOLOGY OF TRAUMA AND DISSOCIATION

Therapy with clients who have experienced severe trauma is often challenging, time-consuming and at times overwhelming. Survivors often have parts who are dominated by implicit memory (unconscious, tenacious, constituted mostly of feelings and sensations with no cognitive input or time sequence). Boiled down to its simplest denominator, the goal of trauma therapy is to convert implicit memory to explicit memory (conscious, factual, linear, with a sense of time and a narrative). The job of all therapists is to help traumatized clients transform raw, undigested memory into a cohesive story that includes feelings and beliefs as well as a beginning, middle and end.

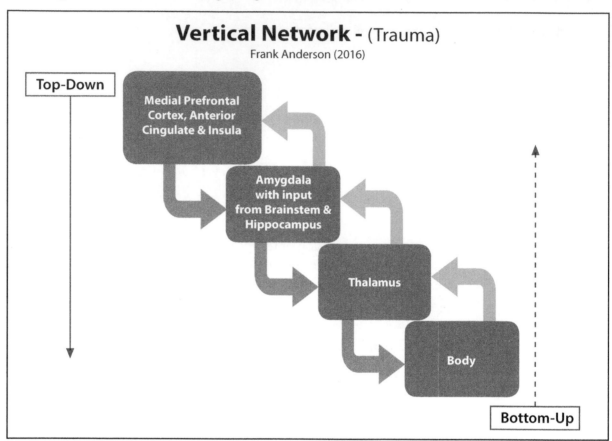

Under normal circumstances when we experience something stressful, the nervous system takes the input from the body and carries it up through various brain structures, including the thalamus (sensory input), brainstem (heart rate and breathing), amygdala (emotional significance), and hippocampus (cognitive input), before going to the anterior cingulate, insula and prefrontal cortex, where the information is processed and the appropriate response – usually calming down – is determined (van der Kolk, 2014).

But when the individual's perception of danger increases because stress is more extreme, chemicals, including cortisol and adrenaline, are released to mobilize the body, moving us from a state of safety to a state in which we are ready for fight or flight (sympathetic activation). In this scenario, the ability to process information and downregulate goes off-line, resulting is a state of high physical and emotional reactivity along with a limited ability to calm down and recover (van der Kolk, 2014).

If we continue to be trapped in a traumatic situation and feel helpless to escape, we move from sympathetic activation to parasympathetic withdrawal and eventual collapse. Here several structures in the brain go offline and internal organs slow down to conserve energy to increase the chance of surviving danger. In this state, we are disconnected from our emotions, our body and our ability to process information (Porges, 2011).

The Three States of Processing Stress

Normal Stress	Sympathetic Hyperarousal	Parasympathetic Blunting
Normal inhibition	Under-inhibition*	Over-inhibition*
Normal thoughts	Little cognitive perspective	Low thinking
Normal emotions	High emotions	Low emotion
Normal body sensations	High body sensations	Low body sensations

* (Lanius et al., 2010)

There are three states that therapists deal with when working with individuals who go through stressful situations. At times, a client is able to process information cognitively, emotionally and physically. At other times (of sympathetic activation) the client is in high emotional and physical activation with little ability to downregulate. At yet other times (parasympathetic blunting) she is numb, dissociated and without access to physical sensations, emotions or thoughts. In the most intense moments, a traumatized client may alternate among all three of these states.

BE WITH YOUR HEART

- *If it feels good, go ahead and take a deep breath and notice your heart in whatever way you experience it – this doesn't have to be your actual heart on the left side of your chest, just however you experience your heart.*

- *I'm going to invite you to get to know it in a physical way and we're going to explore different qualities of your heart.*

- *We'll see about its condition.*
  - *First notice how open it is.*
  - *How tender, encrusted or callused.*
  - *Perhaps it is congested, fluid or flowing.*

- *Also notice how much space your heart has in there.*
  - *Does it feel contracted and tightly packed or spacious?*

- *You might find in your exploration that different places in your heart are different in those ways.*
  - *Maybe the front is closed but the back is open.*
  - *Or the top is tender and the bottom is tough.*
  - *Maybe energy can flow through some parts of your heart but not all.*
  - *Maybe in some places your heart feels pinched and contracted while in other places it feels spacious.*

- *So where it feels extreme in any of those ways – closed, contracted, contested or callused – you have located some protective parts.*

- *If you want, you can take a little time right now to meet those parts.*

- *If it's okay, just get a little curious about what those protectors are afraid would happen if they allowed you to open your heart fully.*
  - *If they let your heart be tender.*
  - *If they didn't try to contract or compact it.*

- *In answer to that question, you are likely to learn about the vulnerable parts they protect who also live in or around your heart.*

  - *Right now you don't have to go to those vulnerable parts, you can just hear a little bit about them from these protectors.*

- *As you get to know how vigilantly these protectors have guarded your vulnerability, just extend your loving appreciation toward them at whatever degree feels sincere.*

- *Notice how they react to that appreciation.*

- *Right now we are not asking them to change anything. Nor do we expect them to change.*
    - *We're just getting to know their fears and showing them appreciation.*
    - *And someday, if they want, if they feel it's a good idea, they may let you go to those vulnerable parts to heal them.*
    - *Then these hard working protectors will be able to relax and allow you to open your heart.*

- *Often protective parts don't believe healing is possible. They feel condemned to do this with your heart for the rest of your life. So just be sure they know it is possible but there's no pressure.*

- *When this visit with your heart protectors feels complete, you can begin to shift your focus back outside but make sure before you leave to thank them for letting you know all this and thank them for their hard work to keep your heart safe.*

THE LAST TWO STEPS IN THE 6F'S:
BEFRIENDING AND EXPLORING PROTECTOR FEARS

The last two of the 6F steps (befriending and exploring a protector's fears) are the way we get to know protectors, understand their motives and concerns (especially about exile overwhelm) and win their permission to help the wounded parts they protect. Finally, in this segment we look at the science of befriending in relation to empathy and compassion and of protector fears in relation to the neurobiology of trauma.

THE 5TH STEP: BEFRIENDING

Once we have found and focused on a target part, fleshed it out and located enough Self-energy in the client ("how do you feel toward..."), we have the opportunity to learn more about the part and foster the relationship between it and the client's Self:

- "What is your job?"
- "How did you get it?"
- "How old are you?"
- "How old do you think the client is?"

- "Who do you protect?"
- "What do you want the client to know?"
- "If you didn't have to do this job, what would you rather do?"

ASKING PROTECTORS ABOUT THEIR MOTIVES

We guide clients to ask protectors about their motives and responsibilities. And we support clients in listening to protectors with respect, interest and an open heart. New practitioners of IFS may have parts who feel daunted by a seemingly unending supply of parts in some clients, however this is not a true obstacle. Parts are like Russian dolls: parts can have parts, who have parts. But we do not ask clients to name all their parts nor do we guide them to have their parts notice subparts. If the conversation goes that way, however, our methods don't change. We focus on the parts who show up – that beehive of protectors revolving around an exile. In this way we are guided by the client's system and we need only learn as much as the system needs us to know to facilitate healing.

BEFRIENDING LEADS TO MORE UNBLENDING

Relationship building is our job throughout IFS therapy. We want parts to be in relationship with the client's Self, which becomes possible when parts make room for the Self inside. As the client befriends protective parts, we concentrate on persuading them to differentiate so the client's Self can be present and embodied.

LISTENING INSIDE

To befriend the client's parts, we focus on building the relationship between them and the client's Self by making sure the client is available to listen and the part feels validated. First and foremost, protective parts need to know that the client understands why they need to do their jobs. We therapists model the attitude that we are suggesting the client cultivate internally: respect for the efforts of protectors, the assumption that their intentions are positive and curiosity about their fears. We are non-judgmental and kind. The premier evidence of the Self (that purely differentiated state) is love, compassion (concern for another's suffering) and the desire to help. We look for this in ourselves and in our clients.

BEFRIENDING A PROTECTOR

(Find)

THERAPIST: I notice a part who overreacts at times. Are you aware of that part?

NAOMI: That's just me. I've been that way for years.

- *The overreacting part is blended with Naomi.*

THERAPIST: I know it feels like that but would it be okay to get curious and ask if this is a part who somehow protects you?

- *Validating and persisting.*

NAOMI: It would be strange to think of this as just some part of me.

- *The idea that a highly reactive part can unblend is a new concept for her system.*

THERAPIST: I know. Can we ask if it's willing to separate from you a little so we can get to know more about it?

- *Validating and persisting.*

NAOMI: I don't know how to do that.

- *Again, unblending is a new concept.*

THERAPIST: I can help. Think of a situation recently where you overreacted.

- *Reassuring and guiding.*

NAOMI: Okay. Last week I found out that my agency wants me to apply for the position of district manager and I freaked out.

(Focus)

THERAPIST: Great, that's exactly what I am talking about. Now even as you focus on that part see if you can get a little distance from it and ask it to tell you about the reaction.

NAOMI: It's funny but I keep hearing "You need to be prepared! Always be prepared!"

- *She has tuned in – or, as we say in IFS, "gone inside" – and listened.*

THERAPIST: Do you know what that's about?

- *Checking to see if she has a general awareness of what motivates this reactive part.*

NAOMI: Not really.

(Feel Toward)

THERAPIST: Want to find out?

- *Checking to be sure she has enough Self-energy toward the part.*

NAOMI: Definitely because I don't know where that came from.

- *She does have enough Self-energy.*

<hr>

(Befriend)

THERAPIST: Great. Let the part know that you're curious and see what it wants you to know.

NAOMI: It doesn't like surprises. Surprises are bad. Really bad!

> • *The first direct communication from this protector.*

THERAPIST: Ask it to say more.

NAOMI: I'm seeing times when my parents, mostly my mother, would scream at me out of the blue when I got something wrong. I was terrified.

THERAPIST: I bet you were. It sounds like this part tries really hard to be sure you're prepared so you won't be surprised like that again.

NAOMI: Yes exactly. I over-prepare with most things and I guess I overreact too when I don't feel prepared. I didn't know this was about her yelling at me all the time.

> • *Rather than being the part (blended), Naomi is now in relationship with the part and therefore able to understand its reasons for reacting strongly to surprises.*

THERAPIST: Let the over-preparing, overreacting part know that we get it and we appreciate how it tries to protect you.

NAOMI: It likes that. It's not used to being appreciated.

❧

As we emphasize throughout this manual, exile overwhelm is the number one fear of protectors. Luckily it is not hard to address.

As this example shows, protective parts can be completely blended. We can say this part is "in the driver's seat" or that the client is seeing the world through its eyes. Helping parts to unblend sets the stage for all other progress in IFS therapy.

BEFRIENDING PROTECTORS

DIRECTIONS: When it's time to listen to inner protectors, be sure that you are available.

Scan internally while asking yourself:

- "How do I feel toward this part of _____ (the client)?"

If the answer is anything along the spectrum from curiosity to compassion, then it's okay to proceed.

But if the answer is anything else, then you have detected a reactive part in yourself. Ask the part:

- "What do you need from me in order to let me listen without judging?" (or being afraid, or whatever reaction you have noticed)

- When a reactive part shows up, validate its experience first.
   - "Of course it makes sense that you feel anxious about _____ [the client] confronting his boss. Would you be willing to dial the anxiety down so we can learn more about your concerns?"

THE SCIENCE OF BEFRIENDING: EMPATHY VS. COMPASSION

Once separation occurs between the target part and the Self, we move to befriending, which we can also think of as internal attachment work. We help the client discover who the part is and what it needs to share: What is its job? How old is it? Who is it protecting?

The mapping of neural networks related to compassion and empathy by neuroscientists helps us understand two distinct ways in which therapists can be with clients: Empathy involves our capacity *to feel with* another person while compassion involves *feeling for* another person and includes the desire to help. While empathy can lead to burnout, compassion leads to resilience (Singer and Klimecki, 2014).

In IFS we view empathy as a (more or less intensely) blended experience in which the therapist or the client's Self feels what the part is feeling. Compassion, in contrast, is an unblended experience with the Self of both client and therapist present with perspective and patience. In the therapeutic journey of establishing trust and connection between parts and Self, parts often need to experience both ways of being in relationship. Together, being felt (empathy) and being helped (compassion) gives them enough comfort and safety to reveal their vulnerability.

THE 6TH STEP: ASSESSING PROTECTOR FEARS

Working with protectors can be challenging because of their reactivity and the potential that they will evoke exiled feelings and activate other protective parts in us or in the client. We need to stay self-aware, be honest about our parts, and tend to those who get activated to minimize their impact on the treatment. Protectors also resist accepting help for any number of reasons and their concerns often require the bulk of our time in IFS therapy. Here is a list of common fears and how we respond.

1. The part will disappear if it isn't needed in this job.
   - We assure the part: "You will not disappear. You are a part of Lucy now and you always will be a part of Lucy. Healing this injury will free you."
2. The therapy will end and the relationship with the therapist will be lost if protectors allow the client's Self to show up.
   - We tell the part: "There is room for Lucy's Self and for me, too."
3. A secret will be revealed.
   - We explore the dangers of this secret, addressing any false beliefs about consequences.
4. The client will be overwhelmed with pain.
   - We assert with confidence that the client's Self has the capacity to handle the part's intense emotions.
5. The therapist won't be able to handle the exiled pain.
   - We stress that this is not true of the therapist's Self and that we will identify and tend to any of our parts who are reactive throughout the therapy.
6. A polarized protector will take over if this part relaxes.
   - We offer to negotiate this with the other protector if it does show up, always getting permission from all parts before proceeding.
7. Self-energy is dangerous and will attract punishment.
   - We explore early experiences of Self-energy being punished, and we introduce parts to the Self slowly so they can experience it at their own pace and over time without bad consequences.

8. There is no Self.
   • We assert that the Self was not destroyed and if parts will relax, it will naturally emerge.
9. The therapist – or other parts – will judge this protector for the damage it has done.
   • We show compassion and assure the part that we will not judge and if critical parts do show up we will address them directly.
10. Change will destabilize the client's inner system.
    • We explore the part's fears and beliefs about change and we assert that the Self will help the system stabilize.

EXPLORING FEARS

Sometimes a protector spontaneously speaks of its fears: "If I let him (the client's Self) in, what will happen to me?" But if not, we make a point of asking about protectors' fears for two reasons.

• First, the fear will point us either toward a polarized protector or it will reveal the exile – and we want that information.
• Second, fearful protectors need help. Until protectors are on board we won't have access to the client's Self or to exiles. So we ask protectors about their fears.

"What would happen if you were to stop doing this job?" There is much to be learned from the part's answer, particularly:

1. If a protector will not relax because it fears emotional overwhelm, we offer to ask the overwhelming part (an exile) to not overwhelm.
   • "I hear that you are concerned about Sean (the client) feeling overwhelmed. That makes sense. We don't want that either. With your permission we can ask that part not to overwhelm."
2. If this protector fears that a polarized protector will get too much influence over the client, we suggest a parlay to get the client's Self between warring parts (Krause, Rosenberg & Sweezy, 2016)
   • "If the part who you're worried about is willing to sit down with you and Sean instead of taking over, would you be willing too?"
   • "Sean, can you hear how each of these parts is trying to help you? Let them know that you value their input and ask if they're willing to trust you enough to make room so all three of you can talk."
3. Finally, if an exiled part is overwhelming the client, the therapist can talk to it directly.
   • "I'm really glad you're here. I see that you're afraid. Would you be willing to make just a little room so Sean can be here, too? If you let him come in with you, he'll help."
   • Note: This is where we urge you to revert to your expertise. Do not try to use IFS with exiles unless you have IFS training.

THE #1 FEAR: EXILE OVERWHELM

The number one concern of protectors is fear of emotional overwhelm. They've seen it happen and they've seen it debilitate the client, often with crippling depressions, anxiety or repeated hospitalizations. We validate their fear and take their concerns seriously. Dealing with emotional overwhelm upfront is one reason IFS doesn't require stabilization before attending to trauma. If overwhelm is not a threat, protectors relax and the client's Self remains present and available.

Validating and Addressing a Protector's Fear of Exile Overwhelm

THERAPIST: Let's thank this part for sharing its concern. Let it know that we can ask the one who feels terrible not to overwhelm.

- *Exiles generally agree not to overwhelm when they realize that separating and being with the Self is the best way of getting attention.*

THERAPIST: Did you hear? The part says it will not overwhelm. Can we talk to it now?

- *Once the exile agrees not to overwhelm, we check back with protectors to get their permission to proceed.*

Here is an example:

Asking an Exile Not to Overwhelm

(Find)

THERAPIST: It seems like you have an anxious part who keeps jumping in, do you notice that?

PETE: Yes, it's having a hard time staying back. It won't stay in the waiting room where we put it.

- *The part is at least unblended enough so that Pete can notice it.*

(Focus)

THERAPIST: Ask what it's upset about.

- *Being curious.*

PETE: It's afraid I'm being taken over.

- *This is the typical protector fear of exile overwhelm.*

THERAPIST: Would it say more?

(Protector Fears)

PETE: It's afraid I'll be taken over by the feelings of the part who was criticized by my football coach. It says we're messing with something I can't handle.

- *This common fear is another way of describing exile overwhelm.*

(Befriend)

THERAPIST: How old does it think you are? And don't filter the answer just say what comes up.

- *His answer will likely reveal the exile, the part who is being protected.*

PETE: It thinks I'm 17 years old. That's when I played football.

THERAPIST: Let's give it a chance to get to know the Pete of today, the Pete who's not a part. Ask it to look you in the eye and let you know who it sees.

- *Eye contact is a great strategy for detecting parts – or the Self. (The authors thank Mike Elkin for this insight.)*

PETE: Wow, it's really shocked. It had no idea that I'm grown up.

THERAPIST: How does it respond to you?

PETE: It sees me but still thinks the feelings are too intense for me.

- *This protector has noticed Pete as a grown-up but is not yet in connection with Pete's Self.*

(Direct Access)

THERAPIST: Can I talk directly to the part who felt criticized by the coach? I'll ask it not to overwhelm.

- *The therapist offers to address the protector's concern (exile overwhelm) by speaking directly to the exile. Alternatively, the therapist could have stayed with introducing the part to Pete's Self and having Pete ask the exile not to overwhelm. Either way is fine but direct access is often faster.*

PETE: That would be great.

THERAPIST: So I want to talk directly to the part who was criticized by that football coach. Are you there?

PETE: Yes.

- *This is the exile speaking.*

THERAPIST: I hear you have some strong feelings, is that correct?

PETE: Yes.

THERAPIST: We can help. If you don't take Pete over, you'll be able to show him what happened and we'll help you to unload this pain for good.

PETE: How?

THERAPIST: If you stop overwhelming Pete, the worried part will be able to relax and then Pete can help you – the Pete who's not a part. Want to try that?

PETE: I'd like to. But I'm not sure I can.

- *Exiles are capable of separating but are not in the habit of doing so voluntarily because they associate separation with being exiled.*

THERAPIST: That's fine. Let's practice.

- *Practice normalizes this new option of being separate yet in relationship.*

PETE: Okay.

THERAPIST: Let's start with you sharing just a little bit of your feelings at a time. Say 10 percent or, if it prefers, a couple of drops.

- *These are two ways in which an exiled part can share its feelings slowly. Another way is to use the image of a volume dial that can be turned up or down. (The authors thank Michi Rose for the "few drops at a time" technique.)*

THERAPIST (continuing)**:** Are you ready?

PETE: Yes.

THERAPIST: Great. Let me check with Pete first. Pete, did you hear that?

> • *Bringing the client's Self in on the conversation.*

PETE: Yes.

THERAPIST: Did the worried part hear, too?

PETE: Yes.

THERAPIST: Are you both ready for this part to share 10 percent of his feelings?

> • *Asking for permission.*

PETE: Yes.

THERAPIST: Okay. Pete and the worried part are both ready for you to share 10 percent of your feelings with him. Go ahead… Let me know when you're feeling it, Pete.

> • *Practicing.*

PETE: I'm feeling it.

THERAPIST: Is this level of feeling okay?

PETE: Yes.

(Befriend)

THERAPIST: Let the part know it's okay so far. What is it like for the part to share this with you?

PETE: A little bit of a relief.

THERAPIST: Great. Is it okay to keep going? Let him know what percentage of the feeling he can share with you now. We can go very slowly. Let me know when you're ready to stop and talk about what it's like for you to be together.

> • *Facilitating the relationship with Pete's Self.*

❧

As this example illustrates, we get permission to talk to the exile so we can ask it to stop overwhelming in return for getting some help. The therapist's Self also helps the client's system feel safe enough to experiment.

SCIENCE: ADDRESSING FEARS AND WORKING WITH EXTREMES

The last step with protectors involves understanding their fear, which is at the core of their resistance to change. We ask, "What are you afraid would happen if you didn't do this job anymore?" because the answer either reveals the wound ("I would be alone") or a polarization ("the suicide part will take over"). When we are too critical or pushy and demanding with protectors their fear will naturally intensify and their behavior will become more entrenched. In this regard, neuroscience can remind us how to pitch therapeutic interventions for best effect.

We find that assessing whether the symptom (the protective part) is rooted in *sympathetic activation* or *parasympathetic withdrawal* is important. For example, rage, panic, flashbacks and binge drinking are generally associated with activation and are rooted in the sympathetic nervous system, whereas numbness, dissociation, and feeling shamed or being highly intellectual are associated with blunting and withdrawal, which are rooted in the parasympathetic nervous system. Some reactions can signify either hyper- or hypoarousal and need to be sorted out before settling on an intervention. For example, a suicidal part can be intense and impulsive (hyper) or quietly looking for an exit to avoid the pain (hypo).

We therapists should always be aware of the reactivity of our own parts and keep them in check. For example, when you are activated do you get nervous or intellectual or controlling? When a client withdraws, do you try too hard? Do you disconnect? Or do you get angry? Whatever you notice about your reactions, if you are able to help your parts relax and trust your Self to be present with the client, good things will naturally unfold.

HANDLING ACTIVATION

As we know, hyperarousal signals danger by mobilizing the body, rousing intense feelings and turning off the areas of the brain that are responsible for assessing, attending, and responding appropriately to our experience. In the face of hyperarousal we should stay calm, rational and non-reactive so that we can help our clients put feelings into words and gain perspective about their present state. When clients are unable to separate from an activated part, we talk directly to the part (direct access) and become the auxiliary brain (the Self of the system), listening to it and addressing its concerns.

This is a *top-down* (accessing the cognitive first then moving toward feelings and, last, physical sensations) approach to a client's sympathetic hyperarousal (Anderson, 2016). We are there to offer a reasonable response, conveying confidence and clarity when she is overwhelmed. We demonstrate strength but we do not try to control her activated part.

If a client has at least some awareness of being activated, he can use out-of-office interventions that feature any number of simple top-down strategies to help him shift states. He can, for example, check his email, watch TV, read a book, or talk to a friend.

We say: "Mainly, when your protective parts are activated don't make decisions or do anything regarding the problem at hand, wait until your brain settles down and your parts can give you the room to have perspective again."

STAYING CALM AND HELPING
AN ANGRY PART UNBLEND

John came to a session angry with his partner and eager to talk about an argument from the night before.

JOHN: I'm so pissed at her! She constantly puts our son Jake in the middle of everything, forcing him to choose between us. Why doesn't she get how destructive this is?

> **THERAPIST:** Sounds hard. And based on your history, I'm guessing this dynamic is particularly challenging for you.
>
> • *Validating.*

JOHN: It makes me want to kill her or kill myself. I can't decide which to do first.

> • *A scared part is activated in the therapist, who silently asks the part to relax.*

(Find and Focus)

> **THERAPIST:** I hear you feel really mad. I wonder if the angry part of you would separate a bit?
>
> • *Asking a hyperaroused part to unblend.*

JOHN: Are you serious? I guess you can't handle my feelings any better than her.

> • *The angry part is unwilling to separate, which is not unusual for angry parts.*

(Direct Access)

> **THERAPIST:** I think I'm talking directly to the angry part, right? That's fine with me. I hear that you're mad because John's son is being put in the middle just like John was with his mom and dad, is that right?
>
> • *Moving right into direct access with the angry part – and John sits back in his chair.*

> **THERAPIST** (continuing)**:** If you can bring the intensity down a bit, I promise he'll come up with a workable solution.
>
> • *Negotiating with the angry part, helping it to separate from John a bit. After a few moments John's shoulders relax and his head tilts.*

JOHN: I know you're right. Thanks for sticking with me.

> • *The angry part has made room for John's Self and his sympathetic activation comes down.*

This vignette illustrates the therapist's need to keep his own parts in-check while helping reactive parts in the client unblend. He moves into direct access to remain Self-led and available to an angry, threatening part who is not immediately willing to unblend. Staying confident and meeting the part head-on without trying to control it, helps it to relax.

Being Calm and Nonreactive When
a Client is Hyperaroused

Noah sits down and immediately begins to describe an interaction with his adolescent son over the weekend.

NOAH: I was so mad at him. I really lost it. I had been very clear about the rules. When we are not home no friends in the house without our permission and absolutely no drinking. I got a call from the police because our neighbor reported noise coming from our house. I was beyond mad.

> **THERAPIST:** I can see how upset you are as you tell the story now.

NOAH: Wouldn't you be angry? I am still so embarrassed.

> **THERAPIST:** Of course that would be upsetting. Let your angry part know that its response makes sense.
>> • *Validating the part.*

NOAH: I'm glad you get it.

(Find and Focus)

> **THERAPIST:** If the angry part is willing to separate just a little bit we'll be able to hear it even better.
>> • *Unblending*

NOAH: You aren't afraid of my feelings?

> **THERAPIST:** Not at all. I know your feelings have important information for us.
>> • *Continuing to validate the part. After a moment, Noah's voice and body posture soften.*

NOAH: No one could tolerate my feelings when I was a kid. I would never hurt anybody. I just feel things intensely.

(Befriend)

> **THERAPIST:** Let the angry part know that its feelings are fine with us and we want to hear all about it.
>> • *Welcoming a part who alarms others and has experienced disapproval.*

⤙⤚

Angry parts are particularly sensitive to rejection - and used to it. But, as this example illustrates, they calm down and are often grateful when they are welcomed with genuine concern and interest.

ACCESSING THE COGNITIVE MIND WHEN A CLIENT IS HYPERAROUSED

The therapist goes to the waiting room to get Tina for her 1:00 pm appointment. She is clearly anxious. The therapist greets her and as they start heading back to the office Tina starts talking, unable to wait.

TINA: My husband is having an affair!

   THERAPIST: When we get into the office you can tell me more.

TINA: Oh my god, I'm devastated!

   THERAPIST: We're almost there. I want to hear what's going on.
      • *The therapist closes the office door.*

   THERAPIST (continuing)**:** Tell me what's happening.

TINA: I saw a text message on his phone last night from a woman.

   THERAPIST: What did it say?

TINA: I can't wait to see you tomorrow.

   THERAPIST: That's it?

TINA: Yes. Who is this woman? Why is he cheating on me?

(Implicit Direct Access)

   THERAPIST: Let's slow down and figure this out together. Did you ask him about the text?
      • *Rather than asking to speak to Tina's panicked part, the therapist simply begins to speak to the part directly, acting as the Self of the therapeutic system, in contrast to "explicit direct access" in which we ask for permission to talk to the part directly, we call this "implicit direct access."*

TINA: No of course not. Then he'll know I know.

   THERAPIST: Did you see any other text messages from this person?

TINA: No.

   THERAPIST: What makes you sure he's having an affair?

TINA: What else can it be?

(Find)

   THERAPIST: Well, it could be a colleague from work. It could be an old friend or someone your husband plans to meet in a platonic way. Who knows? But I see you have a really activated part and I wonder if it's willing to give you some room?

TINA: How can I relax when my whole marriage is on the line?

> ### Going Inside
>
> **THERAPIST:** I'm hearing that this part doesn't want to relax right now. Can I ask a question? Are you hearing from parts who have a different perspective?
>
> • *Tina listens internally and her body relaxes.*
>
> **TINA:** Well, actually, as I was driving here today it did cross my mind that this could be a misunderstanding.
>
> **THERAPIST:** What does that part want you to know?
>
>
>
> As this example illustrates, even as the perceptions of some parts are seriously skewed by past experiences we can ask for other inner perspectives. Parts who are calmer—along with the client's Self—are there and will be able to contribute their observations once panicked parts get help to unblend a bit.

Top-down strategies for unblending sympathetic activation

1. Provide a rational perspective. Help the client to *make sense* of her reaction.
2. Validate the client's experience and put feelings into words: "I'm guessing you feel…"
3. Be clear, centered and express care (compassion).
4. If these strategies don't help the part unblend, move on to direct access.

(Anderson, 2016)

HANDLING WITHDRAWAL

At the opposite end of the spectrum, when increasing danger activates the dorsal branch of the parasympathetic nervous system, shutting down several key structures in the brain, hypoarousal kicks in and the client becomes disconnected from his body, feelings and rational mind (Anderson, 2016). This signals an increased risk of serious harm.

Hypoarousal, a state of over-inhibition (Lanuis, 2010), calls for a very different set of therapeutic interventions. Originating from lower, more primitive brain structures, hypoarousal can occur on a continuum, with one client having little access to body sensations but still being able to identify emotions and thoughts, to another client being fully disconnected from body and feelings but having access to the intellect (Anderson, 2016). Highly cognitive clients often operate primarily from their intellectual parts but are cut off from sensations and feelings. With hypoarousal we use bottom-up interventions, focusing first on body sensations, next on feelings and finally on beliefs to help these parts unblend.

Here are questions to help you assess a client's level of blunting.

- "Are you aware of your feet touching the floor?"
- "Can you take a deep breath?"
- "Can you look at me?"
- "Can you put into words what you are feeling right now?"

In response to withdrawal we want to give alarmed parts as much time, space and control as they require, because it takes longer to recover from withdrawal than it does to recover from activation (Porges, 2011). If the client appears totally shut down, we again become the auxiliary brain by moving right into direct access, which helps the client shift to a mindful state more quickly.

SLOWING DOWN AND USING DIRECT ACCESS WITH HYPOAROUSAL

When Ariel was in the middle of a session the door to the office opened and a loud voice asked, "Where is Dr. Johnson's office? This is my first time here and I am lost."

Ariel froze, the door closed.

> ### The Therapist is the Self of the Therapeutic System

THERAPIST: Are you okay? Can you hear me, Ariel? Can you look at me?

- *No response, which tells the therapist that her dorsal parasympathetic nervous system is activated.*

THERAPIST (continuing): Can you let me know what's going on inside right now? I see you're struggling. Can you take a deep breath?

- *Ariel's continuing lack of response tells the therapist that she has shut down and is not feeling safe.*

THERAPIST (continuing): Can you move your finger?

- *She does.*

THERAPIST (continuing): Great.

- *Since she can move her body she is not totally offline, the therapist starts talking directly to the part who has taken over.*

> ### Direct Access

THERAPIST (continuing): I'm going to speak to the part who took over. I'm here. I'm with you. I'm not going to push you in any way. We can take as long as you need to feel safe. You're the boss and I trust you.

- *After a few minutes Ariel takes a breath and the therapist knows she's back. She adjusts and looks around.*

ARIEL: I went into the closet. It was dark and quiet and I could hear you in the distance but I thought if I stayed quiet no one would find me.

As we see here, some clients with trauma histories go into a state of parasympathetic blunting in response to threat. We know that a part has taken evasive action inside, and if we speak to it directly, reassuring it without engaging in any kind of pressure, the client will be able to return.

Parasympathetic hypoarousal requires bottom-up strategies that help clients unblend and shift states. Being too active, too involved or too direct may scare the part and cause it to dig in with further disconnection. Out-of-office strategies for hypoarousal are emotion- or body-based, such as going for a walk or run, trying some yoga poses, gardening, having sex, listening to music or watching an emotionally charged movie.

Bottom-up strategies for unblending parasympathetic withdrawal

1. Assess your client's level of withdrawal: "Can you hear me? Can you take a deep breath?"

2. Help clients to *sense* (not make sense of) their reaction by focusing first on the body, then on emotions and last on beliefs.

3. Express connection and nurturance (empathy).

4. Let go of having an agenda: slow down, express trust.

5. If these strategies are unsuccessful, move on to direct access.

    (Anderson, 2016)

THERAPIST'S PARTS WITH
EXTREME PROTECTORS

DIRECTIONS: Try this exercise with a client whose "activated parts" trigger you and with a client whose "blunted parts" trigger you.

Think of a client who triggers you.
- Bring this person up in your mind's eye.
- Put the person into a room that has a window and a lock on the door.
- Stay outside the room, looking at your client through the window.
- Now see the client do the thing that triggers you.

Notice your parts who get activated and write them down here:

_____

_____

See if your triggered parts are willing to separate enough so that you can hear them clearly.

_____

_____

Notice if your client's parts seem activated (hyperaroused) or withdrawn (blunted).

_____

Notice if your parts get activated or withdrawn in response to your client's parts.

_____

Now ask your parts to stand behind you for a moment and watch while your Self stays with your client as her or his parts do the triggering thing.

What was it like for your parts to witness your Self being with your client in that moment?

_____

_____

Would your parts be willing to let you be with your client the next time you see them?

_____

When this feels complete, invite your client out of the room and thank your parts for showing up to share their experience with you.

DIRECT ACCESS

Clients who have experienced extreme attachment rupture often have protectors (and sometimes exiles) who don't trust anyone. These parts frequently hide the Self deeply within or outside the body for safekeeping. To feel comfortable about therapy, they need recognition, control and a direct relationship with the therapist. We know this is the case when protectors won't unblend or refuse to talk, or when exiles repeatedly overwhelm the client.

How Direct Access Differs from Internal Communication

Unlike internal communication, which is a three-way conversation among therapist, client's Self and client's parts, direct access is a two-way conversation. The Self of the therapist speaks directly with the client's target part, asking periodically if the part will permit the client's Self to come into the conversation.

In the two-way conversation of direct access, we don't need to take the first four steps (find, focus, flesh out, feel toward), we simply start with the Self of the therapist talking to a part of the client. When we use direct access we begin at the 5th step: we befriend the part before going on to explore its fears in the 6th step.

How to Do Direct Access

To begin, the therapist asks for permission to speak to the part. For this example we use a dissociative part.

- "Can I talk directly to the part who takes you out?"

The client nods.

- "Great. I want to talk to the part who takes Margaret out. Are you there?"

5TH STEP: BEFRIEND

Then we want to learn about and develop a friendly relationship with the target part.

- "What do you do for Margaret?"
- "How did you get the job of taking her out?"
- "Whom do you protect?"
- "What do you want Margaret to know about you?"
- "How do you feel about doing this job?"
- "For how long have you done this job?"
- "How old are you?"

6TH STEP: FEARS

And, finally, we inquire about protector fears, the prime obstacle to progress in therapy.

- "What are you concerned would happen if you stopped doing this job?"

As we mentioned in relation to eliciting fears when we use internal communication, protectors have a number of typical concerns:

1. The part will disappear if it isn't needed in this job.
2. The therapy will end and the relationship with the therapist will be lost if protectors allow the client's Self to show up.
3. A secret will be revealed.
4. The client will be overwhelmed with pain.
5. The therapist won't be able to handle the exiled pain.
6. A polarized protector will take over if this part relaxes.
7. Self-energy is dangerous and will attract punishment.
8. There is no Self.
9. The therapist – or other parts – will judge this protector for the damage it has done.
10. Change will destabilize the client's inner system.

When we do direct access, we listen until we understand the part's role in the system and then we validate the importance of its work, which was crucial for survival at one point in time no matter how deleterious its effects may have become. Following are three examples of direct access:

- The first illustrates direct access plain and simple.
- The second illustrates how we segue from internal communication to direct access.
- The third illustrates how we use direct access with polarized protectors who refuse to unblend unilaterally.

GETTING TO KNOW A PROTECTOR WITH DIRECT ACCESS

THERAPIST: Can I speak directly with the part who avoids parties?

CLIENT: Yes.

THERAPIST: Okay.

- *Having gotten permission, the therapist now addresses the part directly.*

THERAPIST (continuing)**:** I would like to speak with the part who avoids parties. Are you there?

AVOIDANT PART: Yes.

(Protector Fears)

THERAPIST: What are you concerned would happen if you let Joe go to parties?

PART: First he would embarrass himself and then he would criticize himself for days.

- *The avoidant part is naming other parts.*

THERAPIST: You mean he has a part who would feel embarrassed and a part who would criticize him?

PART: No. I mean he has a part who would be embarrassing and a part who would criticize him afterward.

THERAPIST: I see. What would the embarrassing part do?

PART: Blab. Say too much. Say the wrong thing. Freak people out.

THERAPIST: Would you let Joe find out more about the embarrassing part if it promised not to take him over?

- *The therapist wants to find out more about this embarrassing part. Is it an exile who, looking for help, reveals intimate details about Joe's life to strangers? Is it a protector with an agenda, like trying to recruit people to take care of Joe's exile?*

PART: I suppose so. Though I don't know why he'd bother.

- *The avoidant part clearly has a negative view of the "embarrassing" part.*

THERAPIST: He could help the embarrassing part by finding out if it's protecting someone else or if it needs help.

PART: Hmmm. I hadn't thought of that.

THERAPIST: With your permission I can show Joe how to help the embarrassing part either way. And if it doesn't work you can still avoid parties.

PART: Okay you can try.

❧

In the beginning, trying Direct Access with clients can feel strange and a bit awkward, but it's a great way to learn about protector fears, particularly when we are dealing with protectors who are wary and unlikely to cede any control. As we learn here, Joe's avoidant part also had a keen eye on other extreme parts, so talking to it directly revealed a crucial inner dynamic we were unable to access with internal communication.

MOVING FROM INTERNAL COMMUNICATION TO DIRECT ACCESS

> **Find: Internal Communication**

THERAPIST: You have a part who likes to be in control and sees itself as being you. I sense that part is in the driver's seat right now. Are you aware of it?

   • *Checking on the level to which this part is blended with the client.*

GABRIELA: Not really. It just feels like me.

   • *The part is highly blended.*

> **Turning to Direct Access**

THERAPIST: I hear that. I'm guessing this part is pretty active in your life. I'm wondering if you would be willing to let me to talk to it directly so we can better understand its intentions.

GABRIELA: Sure I guess so. I don't really notice that it's a part.

> **Direct Access**

THERAPIST: Thanks. So I want to talk to the part of Gabriela who runs her daily life and keeps things under control. Are you there?

GABRIELA'S MANAGER PART: Somebody has to be in charge.

THERAPIST: Tell me more about someone needing to be in charge.

GABRIELA'S MANAGER PART: Well, someone needs to step up to the plate and run things.

> **Befriend**

THERAPIST: So you're the part who steps up to run things, is that it?

GABRIELA'S MANAGER PART: Yes someone has to.

THERAPIST: What do you mean someone has to?

GABRIELA'S MANAGER PART: She gets overwhelmed all the time. She has a hard time handling most anything. She just checks out.

THERAPIST: I get it! Sounds like you have an important job. Can you tell me where you are located in, on or around Gabriela's body?

   • *Validating the part and then locating it in the client's body.*

GABRIELA'S MANAGER PART: I'm everywhere. I have to be. But mostly I'm in her head I guess. As I said before someone has to be in charge.

(Protector Fears)

THERAPIST: What would happen if you didn't run things and keep them under control?

GABRIELA'S MANAGER PART: I couldn't even imagine not running things. I've been in charge for so long.

(Befriend)

THERAPIST: I was wondering about that. Do you know when you first took on this job?

GABRIELA'S MANAGER PART: Don't you dare mess up!

THERAPIST: Who said that?

GABRIELA'S MANAGER PART: Her dad yells at her all the time. She did it wrong or she's not as good or as smart as her older sister. He was in the military before he met her mom and he was strict.

THERAPIST: This is really making sense. Let me see if I'm getting it right. You are the part of Gabriela who runs things, keeps things in control, always trying to do the right thing so that the little girl who got yelled at and criticized by her dad won't make any more mistakes. Is that right?
- *Exploring its job.*

GABRIELA'S MANAGER PART: Exactly. Someone had to help her.

THERAPIST: I totally get that. You had a really important role in keeping that little girl from getting in trouble.
- *Validating the part's job.*

GABRIELA'S MANAGER PART: You got it.

THERAPIST: What if I were to tell you that there is another way to solve this problem and that you would not have to keep working so hard? Would you be interested in hearing more?
- *Inviting the part to try something new.*

GABRIELA'S MANAGER PART: I can't even imagine not doing this job for her.

THERAPIST: Well that would be completely up to you. But if you give us access to the little girl, Gabriela can help heal those wounds and keep her safe so you won't have to keep doing this job.

GABRIELA'S MANAGER PART: That would be great but I doubt it's possible.

THERAPIST: I understand. I know how to do it, but I need your permission to access the little girl.
- *Expressing confidence and getting permission.*

GABRIELA'S MANAGER PART: I am open to that.

THERAPIST: Great. I appreciate you sharing all this with me. It is super helpful.

GABRIELA'S MANAGER PART: I'm glad someone was willing to listen.

> (Returning to Internal Communication)
>
> **THERAPIST:** Okay to bring Gabriela back? Gabriela, did you hear all that?
>
> **GABRIELA:** Wow, I did. I had no idea that part was trying to protect that little girl. I appreciate that!
>
> **THERAPIST:** Let her know.
>
> **GABRIELA:** She likes the recognition.
>
> ‽
>
> When we use direct access because a protector is stubborn about staying blended, we have a special opportunity to make friends with it. Even silent parts often speak freely when invited. As we see with Gabriela, the most stubborn protectors are also often the most vigilant and heroic.

USING DIRECT ACCESS WITH POLARIZED PROTECTORS WHO WON'T UNBLEND

Camille's off-and-on boyfriend called from another state one spring day to propose to her. She was walking outside on a lunch break. She described stopping and screaming at him over the phone as pedestrians and colleagues walked by looking shocked and puzzled.

CAMILLE: Who does he think he is?

   • *Camille is blended with the angry part right now.*

(Find)

THERAPIST: Who needs your attention, Camille?

CAMILLE: He is such an asshole. I moved across the country to be with him and now when I'm back here he calls to propose!

   • *The angry part ignores the invitation.*

THERAPIST: This part?

   • *The therapist continues to invite the client's Self.*

CAMILLE: I am so embarrassed. Do you know how many people were in front of my building walking around on Monday. It was a beautiful day. It was lunch hour!

   • *This is a polarized protector, a critic.*

THERAPIST: That part?

   • *The therapist offers another invitation to the client's Self.*

CAMILLE: I'm not going to get that promotion. I might as well have been lying on the ground asking people to step over me.

   • *The critic also ignores the therapist's invitation.*

THERAPIST: I hear two parts who I'm pretty sure we've heard from before. There's the part who is angry with Matthew and there's the part who scolds you for being angry. Which of them needs your attention first?

- *The therapist names the polarity and again invites the client's Self – which of course requires parts to be willing to unblend.*

CAMILLE: He's a no-good son-of-a-bitch. I'm taking his contact information off my phone.

- *The angry part jumps back in. None of these parts is willing to unblend.*

> ### Direct Access

THERAPIST: How about if I speak with these parts directly? I want to talk to the part who is mad at Matthew and the part who criticizes Camille for being mad. Are you both there?

CAMILLE: Yes

THERAPIST: Would you be willing to take turns?

- *The therapist asks them to cooperate.*

CAMILLE: Sure.

> ### Direct Access with Two Parts

First Part:

THERAPIST: I want to talk to the part who criticizes Camille first. What are you concerned would happen if you stopped doing that?

- *The therapist chooses to talk to the critic first since the angry part probably will not cooperate until the critic does.*

CAMILLE'S CRITIC: She'd alienate everyone.

THERAPIST: That would be bad. We don't want her to alienate everyone. If she could help the part who feels hurt and she didn't have to get so mad would you need to criticize her this way?

- *The therapist validates the critic's concerns and offers a new option.*

CAMILLE'S CRITIC: She'll always get mad.

- *The critic does not acknowledge the client's Self and seems only to see the angry part.*

THERAPIST: I'm going to talk to the angry part in a minute. But that's not who I mean. I'm talking about the Camille who's not a part. She can help the angry part and the part who feels hurt. Do you know her?

- *The therapist introduces the idea that Camille has a Self.*

CAMILLE'S CRITIC: No.

- *The therapist asserts that the Self can help both protectors equally.*

THERAPIST: How about I talk to the angry part now and then both you and the angry part can meet the Camille who's not a part?

CAMILLE'S CRITIC: Okay.

Second Part:

THERAPIST: Thanks. Now I want to talk to the angry part. Are you there?

CAMILLE'S ANGRY PART: Yes.

THERAPIST: Who do you protect?

CAMILLE'S ANGRY PART: Camille.

THERAPIST: How old is she?

• *The answer "Camille" means the angry part protects an exile.*

CAMILLE'S ANGRY PART: Sixteen.

THERAPIST: So there's a 16-year-old who needs help. With your permission, Camille's core, the Camille who is not a part can help her. Then you won't have to work so hard. Would that be good?

• *The therapist validates the angry part's concerns and offers a new option.*

CAMILLE'S ANGRY PART: Yes.

Sometimes polarized protectors simply take turns blending as they argue. The result can look to the casual observer strangely like an argument between two people in conflict who are somehow housed in the same body - which, from the IFS perspective, is the case.

Once Camille's polarized parts agree, they can meet her Self and – moving into internal communication – Camille can help heal the exile so both parts can let go of their protective roles.

Embodying a Part

DIRECTIONS: First find a protective part to check in with and try direct access on yourself by embodying this protector.

Invite the part to embody and show you what it does for you.

- The part may want to move in a certain way.

- It may want to speak (or sing, shout…).

- It may have a particular posture or facial expression it wants you to notice.
  - Ask the part if you're getting it right.

Ask how long it has helped you in this way.

Ask what would happen if it didn't do this job for you.

Ask the part if you are fully getting its role or is there more.

Ask if you can help the part it protects.

DIRECT ACCESS

DIRECTIONS: Direct access is a two-way conversation in which the Self of the therapist speaks directly with the client's target part, periodically asking if the client's Self can be brought in on the conversation. In direct access, the therapist speaks to the part.

You can use direct access with clients or, for practice, you can conduct a role-play with a colleague or embody one of your client's protective parts by going back and forth between being the therapist and the client, either changing chairs or shifting a bit to one side and then the other on a couch. Try this exercise with a protector.

1. "I want to talk to this protective part directly. Are you there?"

   _____

2. "What do you do for_____ [Marianne]?"

   _____

   _____

3. "How long have you had this job?"

   _____

   _____

4. "How's it going?"

   _____

   _____

5. "What are you concerned would happen if you stopped?"

   _____

   _____

6. "If we could help that part (the one who would take over and do something problematic if this part were to stop), would you still need to do this job?"

   _____

   _____

7. "Have you met the _____ [Marianne] who's not a part?"

_____

_____

8. "Would you like to meet her? She can help you and the parts you're worried about."

_____

_____

9. "Will you give _____ [Marianne] permission to help the part you're worried about if it agrees not to take her over?"

_____

_____

OUR INVITATION TO PROTECTORS

Whether we use internal communication or direct access, once we have gone through the 6F's with a protector, we expect it will feel that the client's Self has a good sense of its job and its fears. If we have succeeded thus far, we have a relationship with the part and we can offer it an alternative solution to the underlying problem of the exile. Our invitation to hard-working protectors, whose efforts have usually brought mixed results at best, is to *try something new.* As incentive, we assert that the part's *risk in trying something new will be minimal* ("you can always go back to doing what you do"), the *wound can be healed* and *the part can be safe* with the client's Self.

WHAT WE SAY TO PROTECTIVE PARTS

"If this little girl no longer felt the pain of being alone in the world would you need to protect her?"

"There is a way to heal her. And once she is healed you would be free to do other things. Are you interested?"

Protective parts usually welcome the opportunity to give up the roles they were forced into once upon a time. We assure them that rather than wanting to get rid of them we want to help them get rid of their jobs. In this way, we offer them a new possibility and hope for a different future.

THE 6F'S GOAL

First we *find, focus* on and *flesh out* a protective part in order to help it unblend and notice the client's Self. Next we ask how the client feels toward the target part in order to help other parts unblend so the client's Self is available. Finally we *befriend* the target part, explore its *fears* and *invite* it to try something new. Our goal with protective parts is to get their permission to access and heal exiled parts.

Common Challenges in the Alliance with Protectors

WHEN BREAKS IN CONTINUITY ARE FUELED BY PROTECTOR FEARS

Often protective parts try to derail the work by distracting. Remember, they are trying to keep the exile out of mind. If this happens and the client forgets what happened last week or a protector changes the subject to avoid returning to a part from the week before, we treat it as an opportunity.

A PROTECTOR OBJECTS TO CONTINUITY

THERAPIST: I hear you have a part who would prefer not to go back to the part (name or describe the part: the little girl, the little boy, the fluffy bird…) who we were talking to at the end of our last session. Is that right? Would it be willing to say why?

- *If it is worried about the client being overwhelmed by the part from last week, then:*

THERAPIST: I see. That makes sense. I wouldn't want that to happen either. If the little girl (little boy, fluffy bird…) agrees not to overwhelm, would it be okay to talk to her (him, it) again now?

- *If the part says it doesn't seem important anymore, or something else seems much more important, then:*

THERAPIST: I see. But I am curious. Can I ask what is most important about paying attention to _____ (the client's current concern) this week?"

> Whatever Happens, Be in Self

If the client replies that the current concern is pressing and needs immediate attention (a decision must be made, a response is required, etc.), then, especially if it doesn't happen all the time, you may choose to follow along.

- Check your Self-energy when you are in this kind of negotiation to be sure you feel Self-led.
- And if you do decide to go along, first ask the client to check in with the target part from the week before to ask how it's doing, get it's permission to shift topics, and set the intention to return to it the next week – and then follow through.

> Help Hard Working Protectors

But if the client has a chaotic life that is chronically interrupted by current crises, keep negotiating. In this case, actively selling the generic goal of IFS therapy to the client's protectors (being what Schwartz calls a "hope merchant") can be a good idea.

(Hope Merchant)

THERAPIST: I have a lot of experience helping clients to help their most vulnerable parts feel better – and then all their hard working protective parts feel better, too.

• *Then validate the fears of the client's protectors.*

THERAPIST (continuing)**:** I know it can be really scary for protectors to let you get near a vulnerable part.

• *And finally reassure.*

THERAPIST (continuing)**:** But we can do this safely. If they are direct with you then we can address each concern. Would they be willing to tell you what the worry is?

(Protector Fears)

If the part who wants to change the subject remains insistent, it's also a good idea to validate its sense of imperative.

THERAPIST: I know your life still has a lot of ups and downs and many interactions with people today cause you to feel unsafe. You have parts who bring you to therapy to fix this problem. But in their view that does not mean hanging around with parts who feel bad and threaten to overwhelm you. Am I in the ballpark?

(If the Answer is Yes)

THERAPIST: Do the parts who bring you to therapy to handle all of these ups and downs know you, the Sally who is not a part?

• *Focusing on introducing the system to the client's Self.*

(If the Answer is No)

THERAPIST: Okay. Then I must be missing something important here. Would it be okay for us to be curious for a moment about why it's hard to promise continuity between sessions to a part like the one from last week?

• *Observing the phenomenon of changing topics and being curious.*

✧◝◟◞

Persistence and curiosity are key to responding when protectors take evasive action. Assume they have legitimate concerns, which they will (eventually) share if you are open-minded and open-hearted with them.

POLARIZED PARTS

Protective parts view vulnerability and the emotional pain of feeling unlovable as the problem. Some parts work proactively to prevent this pain from reaching consciousness; others work reactively to suppress and distract once the pain has reached consciousness. Either way, as they try to solve the problem of emotional suffering they routinely come up with contradictory strategies and get into disagreements. We call parts who disagree over how to hide or manage vulnerability "polarized protectors" – each tries to influence the client's behavior in different directions.

We know what these parts share: both are trying to solve the problem of emotional pain, both are failing and both stand to gain if we can offer an effective new option. Consequently, we can afford to be hope merchants: we really do have an option that will solve their problem and allow them to retool.

NEGOTIATING BILATERAL DISARMAMENT WITH POLARIZED PARTS

Ask your inner system:

- "Please let me hear all opinions about this problem, taking turns. I will write down what you say."

Write down everything you hear, noticing contradictions or disagreements (polarities).

_____

_____

_____

Ask these parts:

- "Which part, or team of parts, needs my attention first?"

_____

_____

Then go back to the cornerstone question:

- "How do you feel toward [the target part]?"

_____

_____

If the answer is a C word that indicates Self-energy (see 8C's in glossary), then proceed with interviewing the target part using the 6F's. If the answer is anything else, then another part is reacting. Help that part unblend (differentiate) so that you can interview the target part.

HANDLING THE POLARITIES OF EXTREME PROTECTORS

Often the external environments of trauma survivors are unstable and chaotic. But when protectors are extreme even though the client's life seems stable, we can surmise that something inside feels dangerous. We do not expect or demand trust from extreme protectors – we ask them for the opportunity to earn their trust. Our goal is to persuade extreme protectors to try something new – with the key word being *persuade*. Since these parts are already feeling pressured to change internally, they are hypersensitive to outside efforts at control. To win their interest, we start by validating: "I understand why you do what you do;" and we abdicate control: "You are the boss."

At the same time, we reassure vigilant parts:

- "You are not your job. If you stop doing this job you will still exist and you would be free."

We also invite:

- "If you didn't have to do this job anymore, what would you rather do?"

We offer hope:

- "With your permission, we can help the vulnerable part to stop overwhelming."

And we make an offer:

- "I can show you an effective alternative that comes with a lot of benefits – all you have to do is meet the client's Self."

Throughout, our challenge is to be with any of our own parts who get stirred up by the client so that we can remain clear and confident. In addition, if an extreme protector (for example, the client is clearly dissociating or reports that everything is blank) won't relax and separate because it believes the client is an endangered child, we can move to direct access ("Can I talk to this part directly?"). We often use direct access with clients who have been diagnosed with dissociative identity disorder (DID), which we in IFS see as a series of extreme polarities that share the goal of keeping feelings and the Self out of awareness at all costs.

TWO EXAMPLES OF POLARITIES

Before we zero in on the exile, IFS therapy tracks relationships between protectors. Here are two different examples, the first illustrates a polarity between two protective parts; the second illustrates a polarity between the protector of a 4-year-old and a teenage part who has her own agenda.

WORKING WITH POLARIZED
PROTECTORS WHO WON'T UNBLEND

When one protector doesn't want the client to hear from another protector, it will interfere. Jeremy's conflict, illustrated below, is between a pot smoking part and a worrying part.

Feel Toward

THERAPIST: How do you feel toward the part who worries, Jeremy? It's especially worried about you smoking pot these days, isn't it?

JEREMY: I hate that part.

> • *A reactive secondary part, probably the pot smoker.*

Protector Fears

THERAPIST: Okay. If the one who hates it were to relax and let you talk to the worried part, what is it concerned would happen?

JEREMY: The worried part would take over and worrying would be my life!

> • *A polarity between the worried part and the pot smoker.*

THERAPIST: And then what?

JEREMY: All work, no play! Anxious. Boring.

> • *The pot smoker is blended.*

THERAPIST: Is this the pot smoker talking?

JEREMY: Yeah. I guess so.

THERAPIST: If the worried part were to agree not to take you over, would the pot smoker let you be curious and find out more about its worries?

> • *Negotiating for both sides of the polarity to unblend simultaneously.*

JEREMY: The pot smoker says that will never work. It's either him or me.

Hope Merchant

THERAPIST: I'm confident it's worth asking the worried part not to take over. Will the pot smoker give us permission?

> • *Being persistent and persuasive.*

JEREMY: It says okay. Suit yourself.

THERAPIST: Great. So ask the worried part if it's willing to not take over if the pot smoker relaxes, too.

> • *Asking a part not to overwhelm.*

JEREMY: It says yes, but it's going to stay close and watch.

THERAPIST: Great, then let's invite them both to sit down with you at a conference table. Make sure you're there with them rather than seeing yourself with them.

- *Checking to see if the client's Self is present.*

JEREMY: I see myself at the table with them.

- *This is a "Self-like part" – a protector who stands in for the client's Self.*

THERAPIST: Okay. Ask the part who's sitting in for you to move over one and let you be at the head of the table. Is that okay?

JEREMY: It's not sure who I am.

> The Client's Parts Don't Know the Self Yet.

THERAPIST: Let's introduce you. But you can only be there if this part – and the other two parts – let you. It's up to them. Are they willing?

- *Being persistent and persuasive.*

JEREMY: Okay. It moved over and I'm there with the three of them.

> Find

THERAPIST: Great. Ask who needs your attention first.

- *Ceding control to the client's parts.*

JEREMY: The worried part.

> Feel Toward

THERAPIST: How do you feel toward the worried part now?

JEREMY: I feel curious. What's it so worried about?

- *The client's Self is now available.*

೧✑౨

The scenario illustrated here is very common. When we help polarized parts we are, in essence, doing couple therapy with two parts who are in a heated argument that may have gone on for years. Additionally, we see in this example that Jeremy has an active Self-like part who inserts himself initially in the place of Jeremy's Self. This, too, is common. When a hot conflict stirs up inner fears, it can seem to protectors like no time to try something new. Our job is to argue just the opposite.

EXPLORING A POLARITY BETWEEN THE PROTECTOR OF A YOUNG EXILE AND AN EXILED TEENAGER

Georgiana came to therapy because she had fallen in love with a woman in her law firm and was considering ending her marriage – which she had not yet told her wife. They had one son in high school and another in college.

GEORGIANA: I'm losing my mind. My job is to take care of my family. I have children. But Ellen and I don't have a sexual relationship anymore and I'm in love with someone else.

[Find]

THERAPIST: Okay, who needs your attention first? The one who takes care of the family or the one who's in love?

GEORGIANA: In love.

[Feel Toward]

THERAPIST: How do you feel toward that part?

GEORGIANA: I feel sorry for her.

THERAPIST: What does she want you to know?

GEORGIANA: Life is short.

THERAPIST: Anything else?

GEORGIANA: She really means it. Life is too short not to live to the fullest.

THERAPIST: Do you understand?

GEORGIANA: Yes.

[Flesh Out]

THERAPIST: Can you see her?

GEORGIANA: Yes.

THERAPIST: How old is she?

GEORGIANA: She's 18.

THERAPIST: What is her relationship with the part who takes care of the family?

GEORGIANA: They don't agree.

 • *That is, the caretaking part, a protector, is polarized with the teenager, who has been exiled in her relationship with her wife. The therapist assumes the caretaking part protects another (probably younger) exile.*

THERAPIST: Okay. I get that. They don't agree. Can we talk to the caretaking part now?"

> • *The therapist's goal is to befriend both sides of this polarity and convince both to unblend so that Georgiana can find out why the caretaking part works so hard.*

GEORGIANA: Okay.

(Feel Toward)

THERAPIST: How do you feel toward your caretaking part?

> • *Assessing her level of Self-energy.*

GEORGIANA: What kind of lawyer would I be without her? I love her.

THERAPIST: How does she respond?

GEORGIANA: She likes that.

(Befriend)

THERAPIST: Tell her you're here to help.

GEORGIANA: She's shaking her head. She can't imagine what I have to offer.

> • *This part does not yet know Georgiana's Self.*

THERAPIST: How old does she think you are?

> • *The answer to this question will tell us about the exile who she protects.*

GEORGIANA: Well, she thought I was a little kid but now she's not so sure.

> • *Georgiana's caretaking part is now beginning to see the Self rather than the little kid she protects.*

THERAPIST: Would she like to find out more about you?

> • *Befriending will help the protector to see Georgiana's Self.*

GEORGIANA: Okay.

THERAPIST: Ask her to look you in the eye and tell you who she sees there.

> • *Eye contact is often a powerful way of detecting blended parts and introducing the Self.*

GEORGIANA: Oops. She's mad at me.

THERAPIST: Say more.

GEORGIANA: She's saying "Where have you been?!"

> • *This response confirms that the caretaking part sees the Self.*

THERAPIST: And what do you say?

GEORGIANA: I'm sorry I wasn't there when she needed me. I didn't mean to leave her alone.

THERAPIST: What was it like for her to be alone?
  * *Finding out more about her experience.*

GEORGIANA: She had to act like she wasn't scared.

THERAPIST: What was hardest about that for her?

GEORGIANA: She was alone.

THERAPIST: Do you get that, Georgiana?

GEORGIANA: Yes. It was a scary time.

THERAPIST: Who does she protect?
  * *Clarifying the caretaking part's protective role.*

GEORGIANA: A 4-year-old.
  * *This is the exile who is being protected by the caretaker.*

THERAPIST: And how old is the caretaker?
  * *The therapist asks this question because protective parts are often close in age to the parts who they protect. Sometimes a protector will say it is "old," which often means it has been around since the part it protects was hurt many years ago.*

GEORGIANA: She's like… 8 years old.

THERAPIST: If you could take care of the 4-year-old instead of her, what would she rather do?
  * *Introducing the idea that this protector will be liberated along with the 4-year-old.*

GEORGIANA: She likes playing soccer.

THERAPIST: Great. So we can help her do that.

> **Protector Fears**

GEORGIANA: She doesn't think so.
  * *This is a typical initial response from a protector.*

THERAPIST: What does she think would happen if she didn't do this job?
  * *Eliciting fears.*

GEORGIANA: Chaos. My life will be ruined. No one will like me.
  * *This is the fear – it was valid once.*

THERAPIST: She makes sure people like you?
  * *Stating the part's job succinctly.*

GEORGIANA: Yes.

THERAPIST: What happens if someone doesn't like you?

- *Exploring protector fears.*

GEORGIANA: It's not okay.

THERAPIST: What's the worst thing about it?

- *Eliciting the part's specific fear.*

GEORGIANA: I'll be alone.

THERAPIST: We don't want you do be alone, either. What do you say to her?

- *This question will reveal how unblended Georgiana is now from the caretaking part.*

GEORGIANA: I know she had reason to be afraid but I'm grown up now and we won't be alone. I'm thanking her for working so hard.

THERAPIST: Does she want your help?

- *Getting permission to help her.*

GEORGIANA: It would be a relief but she doesn't think I really know what I'm up against.

- *Still on protector fears.*

THERAPIST: Would she be willing to get to know you better?

- *Focusing on the part being in relationship with the Self.*

GEORGIANA: She's not sure what the point is but she's willing.

THERAPIST: If she's willing, she doesn't have to believe in anything. This is just an experiment. She can always go back to what she does so well – making sure people like you.

- *Making the offer of change low risk and low cost.*

GEORGIANA: Okay.

THERAPIST: Great. And will she please let you know about any concerns she has along the way?

- *Inviting vigilant parts to object proactively so they feel welcome and included.*

GEORGIANA: But now the 18-year-old is saying "Hey! What about me?"

- *A mistake: the therapist should have checked in with this part as well to reassure her and get permission to proceed with the exiled little girl.*

THERAPIST: I'm sorry. I forgot to check with her. Is it okay with her if you help the 4-year-old?

- *Asking for permission.*

GEORGIANA: How would that help her?

THERAPIST: Would it be good for her if the 4-year-old and the 8-year-old felt safe?

- *Pointing out potential gains for the teenager if she cooperates.*

GEORGIANA: Yeah. It would be good.

THERAPIST: And you can help her, too. What does she need from you?

• *Facilitating the relationship between the teenager and the Self.*

GEORGIANA: Well, she's in love. She wants everyone to get out of her way.

THERAPIST: Do you get that?

• *Not taking a side but continuing to facilitate the relationship between the Self and the teenager before returning to the conflict between teenager and the caretaking part.*

GEORGIANA: I do. I think she's a lucky duck.

Georgiana's presenting problem is an intense inner disagreement about a life-changing decision. The parts involved have strong opposing ideas about what is best for her (they are polarized). One part (Georgiana's caretaker) has exiled the other part (the teenager) because she feels threatened by her sexuality and passion. The caretaker has also exiled the vulnerable 4-year-old part who she protects. We have yet to hear the 4-year-old's story.

The therapist's goals at this point are to convey respect for the perspectives and concerns of the polarized parts, the caretaker and the teenager, and to facilitate their relationships with Georgiana's Self. When they unblend and Georgiana has the opportunity to heal the 4-year-old, the IFS therapist trusts Georgiana will be able to sort out her love life.

INTRODUCING A PROTECTOR
TO THE SELF

DIRECTIONS: Think of some situation that has occurred during your life in which you felt threatened and had the impulse to defend yourself – this does not have to be something extreme. It can be recent or from the more distant past.

Take a moment to imagine yourself back in that moment in time.

- You will have an action urge - notice where it is located and what your body wants to do.
  - If you are alone and feel comfortable moving, go ahead and make that gesture.
  - Or picture yourself making that gesture in your mind's eye.
    - ◊ Repeat the gesture a few times.

Ask your protector how long it has been doing this job. Write down what you hear.

_____

_____

Ask your protector what it believes would happen if it stopped doing its job. Write down what you hear.

_____

_____

Ask your protector who it protects. Write down what you hear. Sometimes protectors are reluctant to share who they protect. Don't push them, find out what they need in order to trust you more.

_____

_____

If it did share who it protects, set an intention to do so, write that down here and work with the vulnerability in a way that is familiar to you.

_____

_____

If your protector is uncomfortable sharing with you who it protects, stay curious (or, if you are not curious, help reactive parts to differentiate) and inquire about what they need to trust you more.

- If it says something along the lines of: "You will be overwhelmed by that vulnerable part," thank it and ask for permission to communicate with the part about not being overwhelming.

  - Then ask the exile if, in return for getting the attention it needs, it would be willing to stay separate and and not overwhelm.

- If it says: "You are not capable of helping that part" ask it if it would be willing to try an experiment to get to know you better.

  - Ask it how old it thinks you are.

  - Ask it if it is willing to meet the you of today, your Self.

  - Give it time to check you out and get to know you.

  - See if it is willing to look you in the eyes.

  - Ask it, "What is it like to meet me?"

  - And, "Can I have your permission now to help that vulnerable part?"

We all have protective parts who work too hard for us - including the ones who cause us to be "lazy" and unmotivated. In our view, we should declare a yearly national holiday along the lines of Labor Day to honor our protectors, whose efforts on our behalf are often nothing short of heroic. To appreciate the full range of their strategies, here is a list of common protector roles, which by no means exhausts the possibilities.

Introducing A Protector and the Self
- Meet Your Inner Shame Protectors
- Meet Your External Shame Protectors
- Meet Your Compliant Protectors
- Meet Your Anxious Protectors
- Meet Your Dissociative Protectors
- Meet Your Appearance Protectors
- Meet Your Somatizing Protectors
- Meet Your Intimacy Protectors
- Meet Your Food Protectors
- Meet Your Mood-Altering Protectors
- Meet Your Mindfulness Protectors
- Meet Your Sex Addict Protectors
- Meet Your Power Broker Protectors
- Meet Your Success Protectors
- Meet Your Keep-a-Low-Profile Protectors
- Meet Your (exiled) Angry Protectors
- Meet Your Religious Protectors
- Meet Your Political Protectors
- Meet Your Self-Harm Protectors
- Meet Your Suicidal Protectors
- Meet Your Revenge Protectors
- Meet Your Exercise Protectors
- Meet Your Electronic Gadgets Protectors
- Meet Your Intellectual Protectors
- Meet Your Entertainment Protectors
- Meet Your Humor Protectors

Template

MEET YOUR PROTECTOR EXERCISES

DIRECTIONS: Use this template to get to know your protectors. Look over our list of common protector roles and add any we don't mention that are relevant for you.

Notice if this protector is proactive for you (trying to stop feelings from arising) or reactive for you (trying to distract from feelings).

_____

Once you have permission to get to know this protector, ask:

What does it believe would happen if it stopped doing its job? Write down what you hear.

_____

_____

_____

Who does it protect? Write down what you hear.

_____

_____

Ask for permission to help the part it protects.

If it did share who it protects, set an intention to do so, write that down here and work with the vulnerability in a way that is familiar to you.

_____

_____

If your protector is uncomfortable giving you permission to help that part, stay curious.
- Or, if you are not curious, help your reactive parts to unblend and ask why.

If it says something along the lines of: "You will be overwhelmed by that vulnerable part," ask for permission to ask the exile to not overwhelm.
- Then ask the exile if, in return for getting the attention it needs, would it be willing to stay differentiated and not overwhelm.

If it says: "You are not capable of helping that part," ask it if it would be willing to get to know you better.
- Then ask it to look you in the eye and let you know who it sees there.

If it sees a reactive part, take a moment to help that part differentiate.

If it sees some quality of Self, ask, "What is it like to meet me?"
- And, "Do I have your permission now to help that vulnerable part who you protect?"

Meet Your Inner Critics

These parts are our ad hoc continual improvement committee. They are relentlessly vigilant, critical, often humorless and usually unpopular with other parts in the system.

- Ask if any other parts are scared of this critic
- If so, help those parts by listening to their concerns and asking if they would be willing to wait in a soundproof room while you talk to the critic
- Alternatively, you can put the critic into a room and then help the scared parts to relax back and trust you

Meet Your Outer Critics

These parts externalize blame. They use all manner of prejudices that involve "othering" to help us feel acceptable, included, safe and important. They are:

- Racist
- Homophobic
- Transphobic
- Misogynist
- Xenophobic

Meet Your Compliant Protectors

These parts try to keep us connected and in the loop, they often make us think of the welfare of others before letting us take care of ourselves. They are:

- People pleasers
- Caretakers

Meet Your Anxious Protectors

These parts want to forestall negative surprises, they want to be sure we don't get hurt and we don't fail, they want to be sure we're not oblivious or naive and innocent. They are:

- Anticipatory
- Often very physical
- Hard to ignore
- Alarmed about imaginary catastrophes
- Full of warnings

Meet Your Dissociative Protectors

These parts take us out either to prevent or to suppress the negative feelings of exiled parts or the reactivity of other, more extreme protectors. They do things like:

- Cloud the mind
- Take us out of time and awareness completely
- Interfere with our ability to hear what others say
- Interfere with our ability to notice danger
- Numb the body so we don't feel that little electric shock with each reminder of frightening experiences

- Ally with parts who take prescribed medications to dull the nervous system
- Ally with parts who self-medicate with illegal drugs or alcohol
- Ally with parts who numb the body with food

Meet Your Appearance Protectors

These parts keep us focused on how we look to others. They want us to have attention, approval, safety and love. They do things like:

- Criticize our looks
- Invite others to criticize our looks
- Encourage us to go shopping
- Fantasize ideal scenarios
- Warn us about negative scenarios
- Obsess over clothing and material goods
- Haunt the mirror

Meet Your Somatizing Protectors

These protectors use the body to get our attention, to influence our behavior, to get attention for us from others, to try to communicate something important about our past experience or the nature of our pain, and generally to promote their agendas. They do things like:

- Give us migraine headaches
- Make us feel nauseated
- Make us hypersensitive to smells
- Make us feel exhausted
- Amplify asthma and allergic reactions
- Give us chest pain

Meet Your Intimacy Protectors

These parts manage and regulate closeness in relationships to protect us from being too vulnerable and getting hurt. They do things like:

- Cultivate an angry edge that keeps us from wanting to be close to anyone and vice versa
- Act needy and overly attached
- Act overly sexual
- Act disinterested
- Act sleepy
- Act bored and disengaged
- Daydream when someone else is talking
- Ally with parts who focus on food or alcohol in social settings
- Ally with parts who focus on electronic gadgets

Meet Your Food Protectors

These parts obsess about food, either indulging or restricting as a way of distracting us from noticing exiled feelings or suppressing those feelings when they come up strongly. They do things like:

- Feel hungry
- Long for and obsess about certain comfort foods
- Overeat
- Restrict
- Fear and avoid certain foods
- Feel sick after eating certain foods
- Restrict calories
- Binge
- Purge

Meet Your Mood-Altering Protectors

These parts use mood-altering substances, legal or illegal, to numb, avoid or distract us from emotional pain and inner conflict. They do things like:

- Drink alcohol
- Smoke pot
- Snort or smoke cocaine
- Take ecstasy and other party drugs
- Snort or shoot heroin
- Sniff glue
- Take prescribed mood-altering pills
- Take unprescribed (or prescribed) mood-altering medication

Meet Your Mindfulness Protectors

These parts use meditation to bypass threatening feelings, fill a sense of emptiness, or as a facsimile for dissociating. They do things like:

- Encourage us to disconnect from all thoughts and feelings
- Dissociate
- Keep our mental processes abstract or vague
- Distract us from emotional pain with hyper- or hypo-focusing
- Encourage us to be stoic
- Encourage us to think instead of feel

Meet Your Sex Addict Protectors

These parts are adept at seduction and spend their time recruiting lovers to pack inner emptiness with drama and attempts at connection. They focus on:

- Sexual attraction
- Longing and desire
- Games of seduction
- Passionate sex when reuniting after quarrels (make-up sex)
- The physiologic release of orgasm

Meet Your Power Broker Protectors

These parts are into power. Their goal is to dominate. They love being in control. They do things like:

- Keep vulnerability out of sight at all costs
- Blame vulnerable parts for getting us hurt
- Attack and shame other people who display vulnerability

Meet Your Success Protectors

These protectors want us to become rich or successful, to feel admired and never feel rejected. These parts do things like:

- Promote a grandiose sense of our value inside and interpersonally to counter the worthlessness of our exiles and the shaming of our inner critics
- Promote the idea that failure is terrible
- Deny mistakes or failure
- Punish others - particularly our children - for making mistakes or failing
- Avoid apologizing

Meet Your Keep-a-Low-Profile Protectors

These parts do not like us to be seen, to compete, or to threaten others in any way. They keep us invisible, safely under the radar. They do things like:

- Promote the feeling that attention is dangerous
- Avoid letting us be seen
- Discourage ambition
- Refuse to strive for any goal
- Avoid letting us feel good about accomplishments
- Warn us that others will be hurt by our success

Meet Your (exiled) Angry Protectors

Parts who felt angry at mistreatment are often young. They may have stepped forward to protect another young part and been exiled because their anger was unsafe. They often continue to be treated like Kryptonite in the system because anger itself is viewed as a perpetrator behavior. They:

- Smolder
- Resent
- Interrupt
- Push
- Disdain
- Explode

Meet Your Religious Protectors

Some protectors help us overuse religion, idealize religious leaders, long for redemption, long for community, meaning and purpose in life, and care about belonging at the expense of a sense of self and connection to people who are different. These parts:

- Make us feel right
- Make us feel held
- Banish doubt
- Distract from a sense of emptiness and loneliness

Meet Your Political Protectors

Like religious protectors, our political protectors help us find leaders, belong, have community, purpose and structure when feeling empty and alone. These parts:

- Make us feel our side is right
- Make us feel righteous and superior
- Explain right and wrong
- Banish doubt

Meet Your Self-Harm Protectors

These parts cut, scratch, hit and burn to punish, distract, soothe, try to get help, forestall suicide or rage. They do things like:

- Distract from emotional pain
- Shift focus due to the need to tend to injuries
- Concretize emotional pain in blood
- Help us feel alive through pain
- Recruit others to respond to our physical injuries and care for our body

Meet Your Suicide Protectors

The idea of suicide is often a comfort to people who are in extreme pain, emotional or physical. These parts:

- Offer a theoretical (soothing to think about) exit from unending and seemingly insoluble suffering
- Offer an actual (emergency) exit from unending and seemingly insoluble suffering
- Promote the ultimate escape
- Want revenge
- Seek attention
- Want others to react or rescue

Meet Your Revenge Protectors

When we are mistreated, rendered helpless by someone more powerful, humiliated, or made to feel worthless one common response is to want revenge. These parts:

- Are vindictive
- Use sarcasm to gain power
- Try to even the playing field
- Humiliate anyone who feels threatening
- Preoccupy us with fantasies of being powerful and taking revenge, which in the extreme can include hurting or killing someone else

Meet Your Exercise Protectors

These parts often work in conjunction with parts who obsess about our appearance. They can also pinch hit for eating disorder parts. They do things like:

- Hound us to exercise
- Hyper-focus on health
- Urge us to achieve new fitness goals
- Become panicky when we are ill or injured
- Critique the body for imperfections
- Admire bodies that are shown in fashion or sport magazines

Meet Your Electronic Gadgets Protectors

We now have a whole new dimension, a veritable looking-glass world, into which we can fall for endless distraction. Since for most people work and communication depend on electronic instruments like cell phones and computers, our parts who seek to distract us in this way operate virtually no holds barred with endless options. These parts do things like:

- Take us out when we are at the office
- Take us out when we stand in a line
- Take us out when we are in unpleasant environments like airports, elevators, and busy, noisy public streets
- Take us out when we are in conversation

- Take us out at meals
- Take us out in school, at lectures, in libraries
- In short, they are available to take us out anywhere, anytime

Meet Your Intellectual Protectors

These parts flourish in families and settings that celebrate and survive on the cognitive strengths (e.g., the child of a professor who grows up in a university town). They do things like:

- Think as a way of overriding or interrupting feelings
- Look down on people who don't rely on thinking parts as much
- Help us feel special
- Value knowledge and achievement over feelings and intuition

Meet Your Entertainment Protectors

Netflix anyone? The human mind is engaged by stories, whether they are banal and cliched or original. Our electronic devices deliver an endless stream of visuals, words, music, real and fictional stories. These parts do things like:

- Take us out to the movies, watching TV, cable or various other subscriber services
- Live vicariously through movie characters and retell the stories of the shows we have just watched
- Provide false hopes via reality TV
- Relate to the characters depicted therein to learn, emulate and make sense of experience

Meet Your Humor Protectors

These parts use humor in all kinds of ways to set a tone and influence others. They do things like:

- Keep others happy and engaged
- Please
- Entertain
- Get attention for us
- Provide a distraction from painful or uncomfortable moments
- Cover up feelings
- Distract from feelings internally
- Injure others so they will move away from us
- Exact revenge

Exercise

AN ENDLESS SUPPLY OF
PROTECTIVE STRATEGIES

DIRECTIONS: The protectors who often show up in traumatized individuals include dissociation, inner and outer shamers, overwork, keeping-a-low-profile, compliance, anxiety, rage, revenge, suicide, sex addiction, mood-altering substances, intimacy-seeking and intimacy-avoidant, eating, exercise, appearance obsession, somatizing, and intellectualizing.

If you notice protectors in your system who are missing from our list, add them below:

_____

_____

_____

_____

_____

_____

_____

_____

_____

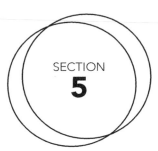

Healing: The Unburdening Process

While we encourage therapists to try working with protective parts using the 6F's (find, focus, flesh-out, feel toward, befriend and explore fears), we discourage therapists from trying to unburden exiled parts without more formal IFS training (for example, an IFS level 1, which are listed at www.selfleadership.org).

Pursuing an unburdening without the appropriate skill level would not be respectful of the client's already fragile system and can easily backfire by causing protectors to mistrust you. If an exile does arise in your work, we encourage you to do whatever you normally do when working with such vulnerability.

However we do illustrate the steps of unburdening below so the reader has an overarching view and is completely informed about the IFS model of therapy. Those who wish to learn to do unburdenings can pursue IFS experientially, in therapy and training.

UNBURDENING AFTER WITNESSING

Healing is set in motion as soon as protectors allow the Self to be in relationship with exiled parts. We may know that access has been granted because the client is suddenly seeing events from the past, or the client may make a more formal agreement with protectors to step back and let the Self see the exile's experiences. When clients are "in Self" you see a shift: their voice gets softer, their body relaxes and their perspective becomes more open and expansive. In either case, as illustrated throughout this manual, we call this step in IFS therapy "witnessing."

During witnessing, an exiled part takes the Self on a tour and the rising memories may surprise the client, who had dismissed or forgotten what the part is showing. The part may show an event that signifies a long pattern of abusive, exploitive or neglectful interactions or it may show a moment of betrayal or terror. In either case, the events it shows will have led to negative consequences (frightening bodily sensations, negative feelings and negative beliefs about safety and self-worth) that need to be disconfirmed in the relationship between the Self and the part. During witnessing, exiled parts have the client's Self with them (compassion), and they may need the client's Self to feel some portion of what they are feeling (empathy), but they are also aware of and need compassion from the therapist too.

THE UNBURDENING PROCESS

1. **WITNESS:** The exiled part shows the Self about its experience.

2. **DO-OVER:** The Self comes into that time and space, and gives the part what it needed and wanted at the time but never got.

3. **RETRIEVE:** The Self retrieves the part from the past and brings it somewhere safe in the present.

4. **UNBURDEN:** The part lets go of toxic sensations, feeling states and beliefs.

5. **INVITE:** The part invites any new qualities it wants or needs for the future.

6. **PROTECTOR CHECK-IN:** Protectors are invited to notice that the part they protected has been unburdened and healed so they can let go of their jobs.

WITNESS

Exiled parts are often shocked to meet the Self. "If you exist, why have I been suffering like this?" In which case, apologies and patience are in order. Once the part feels ready to connect it begins to show and tell the Self about terrifying, shaming, injuring experiences that burdened it and the inner system with toxic beliefs. During witnessing, we ask the client: "Do you see yourself with the exile or are you there?" If the former, a Self-like part has stepped in and we ask that part to let the client's Self take over.

DO-OVER

If the part is stuck in a bad situation, the Self offers to come in and do what the part needed someone to do at the time (restrain an adult, speak up to others, hold the part, love the part, or whatever it requests). Rescripting a traumatic moment with a preferred outcome is very important for some parts. They do not, of course, forget what happened, but the process seems to be validating and emotionally significant.

RETRIEVE

Finally, when the exile signals that its needs have been met and witnessing feels complete, the client's Self invites the exile to leave the past and come with it to the present time in a safe place of its choice.

UNBURDEN

Once the exiled part is safe in the present with the client's Self, we invite it to release any physical sensations, feelings, or thoughts it carries related to the trauma. Here we usually follow the client's lead but if the client asks, we offer suggestions like throwing burdens in the ocean, burning them in a fire or releasing them to the air. (e.g., If it wants, the part could give this burden up to light, earth, air, water or fire.)

INVITE

When the exile lets go of burdens it has more space internally. One of the last healing steps is to instruct the part to invite in any qualities it has been missing. The reply to this very general instruction almost always includes positive qualities that relate to Self-energy, along the lines of love, play, joy, spontaneity, courage, connectedness and creativity.

PROTECTOR CHECK-IN

Once the exile is healed, we invite protective parts to come in and take a look at the part. They often spontaneously let go of their protective role because they see that the part is safe in the presence of the client's Self. In trauma it is common for protective parts to carry their own burdens, which will need to be addressed during a follow-up session.

TRANSFORM

During the process of the Self witnessing, redoing, retrieving, unburdening, inviting and reintegrating vulnerable parts, they are transformed and healed, which gives the whole inner system an opportunity to grow spacious and strong.

THE STEPS OF THE UNBURDENING PROCESS

Hetta came to therapy because she wanted to have children but had overwhelming anxiety about being pregnant. In this interchange she has gotten permission from her protectors to help a 7-year-old exile.

HETTA: She's so surprised to see me. She's saying, "Where have you been?"

(Befriend)

THERAPIST: What do you say?
- *Checking for Self-energy.*

HETTA: I'm telling her I'm sorry I left her alone.
  - *Hetta has access to Self-energy.*

  THERAPIST: What does she say?

HETTA: She's saying if she didn't deserve it, why did I do it?

  THERAPIST: What do you say?
  - *Letting Hetta's Self take the lead.*

HETTA: I wasn't there. I'm really sorry. But I'm here now.

  THERAPIST: How does she respond?

HETTA: She's looking at me. She wonders if she can trust me.

  THERAPIST: What's it been like for her to be without you?
  - *Helping to keep defensive parts from taking over and avoid telling the part what to feel by orienting the client toward witnessing.*

As this vignette illustrates, in IFS we focus on repairing the relationship between the part and the client's Self until the part feels understood and validated.

(Witnessing)

When the repair is sufficient and the exile has confidence in the Self, the part will begin a virtual tour to show the Self whatever it needs to have witnessed. The witnessing interlude is a kind of bonding and de-shaming (validating) process for the exiled part. Once witnessing is in flow we want to continue until the part is satisfied that the Self understands and the part is ready to unload its burdens. This may require more than one session. Let's continue with this example. Hetta sees the 7-year-old in a hospital room.

HETTA: This is before she had heart surgery. Her mother is crying in the hall with a nurse. Someone walking by in the hall says, "That's the one!" and she thinks it means she's the one who's going to die.

  THERAPIST: What is that like for her?
    • *Witnessing.*

HETTA: Where is her father?

  THERAPIST: He's not there?

HETTA: No. He never came.

  THERAPIST: Can she feel you there with her?
    • *Checking on the Self-to-part connection.*

HETTA: We're walking around the hospital. She hates the smell. She's telling me not to have children because we'll end up back in a hospital and die.

  THERAPIST: What do you say?
    • *Handing the baton to the client's Self.*

HETTA: I can see why she's worried. I'm telling her that I trust my doctor. I'm asking her if she can trust me. She's also afraid if something is wrong with my child I will leave like dad did.

(Witnessing)

  THERAPIST: What does she want you to know about that?

HETTA: She misses her real dad.

  THERAPIST: Do you understand what she means?

HETTA: Yeah. He was there when I got home but he didn't seem like my real dad anymore.

(A Do-Over)

  THERAPIST: Is there anything she needs you to say to him now that she needed someone to say at the time?

HETTA: She wants him to apologize.

  THERAPIST: What does she want you to say to him?
    • *The part directs.*

HETTA: You should have loved your daughter better than that… .

  THERAPIST: What's happening?

HETTA: He says he's sorry. He does love her. He was afraid. She won't forgive him now but she's glad he apologized.

THERAPIST: Does she need anything else to happen with him – or anyone else?

   • *The part directs.*

HETTA: Not now.

THERAPIST: Can you give her what she needed back then?

HETTA: Yes she needed to be loved. I'm doing that now and she really likes it.

(Retrieval)

THERAPIST: Is she ready to leave that time and place?"

HETTA: Yes.

THERAPIST: Bring her somewhere safe in the present time. What's it like for her to be with you now?

HETTA: She likes it. I'm showing her around. I'm asking if she could trust me to take care of a child, even if that child had a problem.

As we see, initiating therapy helped Hetta find a part who felt abandoned in a lonely, terrifying moment. After having had heart surgery, Hetta recovered and her post-surgery parts, eager to look forward and be active, had minimized this experience of illness, fear, anger and imminent death. After Hetta's Self validated her experience of the illness and abandonment and spoke up for her with her father she was ready to leave the past.

(Unburdening)

THERAPIST: Now that she's with you in the present, is she ready to let go of all the thoughts, feelings and sensations she got from that experience?

   • *Inviting the part to let go of fear and toxic beliefs.*

HETTA: Yes.

THERAPIST: Have her show you where they are – in, on or around her body.

   • *Deepening the experience.*

HETTA: She has pins in her heart.

THERAPIST: What does she want to do with them?

   • *The part directs.*

HETTA: She's pulling them out and sticking them in the ground… that let everything out.

THERAPIST: Everything?

HETTA: Anger, sadness. It's blowing away.

(The Invitation)

THERAPIST: With that gone, what would she like to invite in?

HETTA: Strength. Energy. Play!

THERAPIST: How's she doing now?

HETTA: Really good. She looks so peaceful and at ease. That's amazing!

THERAPIST: Invite her protectors to come and take a look. Let them know she is safe with you now. Do any of them have anything to say?

HETTA: Yes, they like it.

THERAPIST: Do any of them need your help with feeling stuck or carrying burdens?

HETTA: I think they do.

THERAPIST: That makes sense. Let them know we'll come back to them next week. Meanwhile, do they need a safe place to be?

HETTA: No, they're okay.

THERAPIST: Will they let you take care of the 7-year-old?

HETTA: Yes. They're okay with that.

Once Hetta's exiled 7-year-old feels understood and validated, and her fears have been addressed, she is willing to trust Hetta's Self and let go of her burdens. At the end of her unburdening, the therapist invites the parts who have protected her to notice what has happened and speak up about any further concerns as well as their own needs.

As Hetta's unburdening illustrates, IFS is a transformational model. Once protectors allow the client's Self to have a relationship with an exile, the Self witnessing the exile's experience heals attachment wounds. When the exile is ready to leave the past, retrieving it formalizes the client's mental shift to the present, which liberates protectors. Finally, unburdening illustrates both the ways in which frightening experiences and oppressive beliefs ("I'm unlovable, I'm worthless") grip the body ("I have pins in my heart") and the wonderfully antithetical benefits of feeling securely attached in the present with the Self.

STEP-BY-STEP BUT NOT ALWAYS LINEAR

As we move through these steps, from befriending protectors to witnessing and unburdening exiles, we can only be as linear as the client's system allows us to be. As we get close to an exile, we expect protectors to get activated. If this happens, the therapist's Self usually steps in to explore their fears, offer reassurance and negotiate a way forward.

LETTING GO: THE MOMENT OF TRANSFORMATION

After the Self witnesses the exiled part's traumatic experiences and the exile is safely in the present, the Self invites the part to let go of traumatic body sensations, toxic beliefs and extreme feeling states. We invite the exile to choose how it wants to let go, and we often suggest choosing one of the elements (light, earth, air, water, fire), an option that unfolded organically over the years as IFS therapists stayed with the wishes of clients' internal systems, which is consistent with the traditions of Shamanism. Letting go is the ceremonial endpoint to the whole process of unburdening. Before proceeding, we make sure all burdens are gone.

WHAT NEXT FOR EXILES?

After unburdening we invite exiles to bring in desired qualities that have been blocked by burdens. Most often they name something in the ballpark of the usual C (curiosity, calm, clarity, connectedness, confidence, courage, creativity and compassion) or P (presence, patience, persistence, perspective, playfulness) words: "I want to play," "I want to be creative," "I want courage," "I want love."

FOLLOWING UP WITH PROTECTORS

After an unburdening is complete, we check with protectors. Did they watch? How do they feel now? Are they ready to retire or retool and have a new job? Sometimes they are ready to change and sometimes they wait to see how things will go before giving up their jobs entirely. But they will in any case express relief and be more relaxed. If the unburdening wasn't complete or (down the road) if a burden comes back, they will stay vigilant.

WHAT NEXT FOR PROTECTORS?

If protective parts are relieved after watching the unburdening and feel ready for change, we ask what they would rather do. Often a protector will choose the opposite of what it has been doing. For example, a critic will want to cheerlead or a cautious part will want to encourage the client to explore. But some hard-working protectors just want a break. In addition, especially in clients with trauma histories, some protectors hold their own burdens and will need help to unload what they carry. Once protective parts have released their burdens or let go of the job they held, their wishes can be surprising. A protector of one client declared its wish to go sailing, at which she burst out laughing and said, "Where on earth did that come from? I don't like boats. I don't even like to swim."

POST UNBURDENING: FUTURE SESSIONS

In the weeks after an unburdening we often hear clients describe various sensory analogs for release like "light," "fizzing" or "serene," and when the client checks in she finds the unburdened part is playing or otherwise happily engaged. We also often hear spontaneous reports from clients who feel what we consider to be unblended and more Self-led: he finds he is calmer; she finds she has more confidence, etc. Whatever liberated protectors have chosen to do, we return to check on their needs and we also ask the client to check in with the unburdened part daily for three or four weeks because this seems to be the time internal systems require to integrate and consolidate change.

WHEN BURDENS RETURN

But obstacles can arise and burdens can be taken back. This is most likely to happen when:

1. A crisis occurs in the client's life right after an unburdening, which frightens protectors.
2. A protector who did not give permission for the unburdening actively undermines it.
3. Lack of follow up by client during the week causes the part to once again feel abandoned.
4. The exiled part did not share its whole story.
5. The burden was not fully understood by the Self.
6. Another part within the system is using the burden.

A Burden Returning

THERAPIST: Will you check-in briefly every day with that part you just healed?

ZACH: I'll try my best.

THERAPIST: What might get in the way?

- *"I'll try my best" is an ambivalent enough response to raise a red flag.*

ZACH: I get busy.

THERAPIST: How about setting a time? When you wake up or go to sleep? It's really important to strengthen this new bond between you and him. It takes about 3 weeks to solidify.

- *We emphasize the importance of checking in with parts who have unburdened for at least three weeks afterward.*

ZACH: Okay I can do that.

(One Week Later)

THERAPIST: Let's check in with the teenage boy you helped last week.

ZACH: I had a bad week. My wife and I got a call from my son's principal. They caught him smoking pot at a school dance. We had a series of meetings and he got suspended. We had to come up with consequences at home. Honestly, I really didn't have time to check in with that kid.

THERAPIST: What happened with Josh does sound preoccupying. Let's check in with your teenager and see how he's doing. Is he still in the present with you on the beach?

ZACH: I can't really tell. I don't see him anymore.

THERAPIST: Take a little time and check around for him inside.

- *If an exile has been dropped after an unburdening, be persistent, follow up and reestablish the connection.*

ZACH: I think he's back in my childhood bedroom.

THERAPIST: Ask him what happened.

ZACH: He got scared about what was happening between Josh and me.

(Witnessing)

THERAPIST: Would he share more about that?

ZACH: I was mad at Josh. He says I was acting a lot like my father so he left.

THERAPIST: Does that make sense to you?

ZACH: Yeah. Now that he points it out. My dad got mad a lot when I was young and we really didn't talk about that last week.

> • *Zach is now getting some space from his "dad" part who was rejecting his own teenager as well as his son.*
>
> **THERAPIST:** Sometimes a wound reopens because the part loses the connection with you or sometimes the part didn't get to share everything. It sounds like a little of both happened for him.
>
> (Repairing)
>
> **ZACH:** I see that now. I'm apologizing to him. I don't actually want to act like my dad.
>
> **THERAPIST:** Would it be okay to hear more from him about your father's anger?
>
> **ZACH:** Yes.
>
> ℰ✄ℂ
>
> We recommend assessing how things are going for the client and the relevant parts after an unburdening. When a burden returns, we'll find out one way or another because it will effect the client negatively. The sooner we catch any problems, the better.

We will not offer any exercises in this manual for unburdening exiles because we urge you to do whatever you typically do with vulnerability if you come across an exile. To learn the steps that help an exile unburden, seek formal training in IFS therapy.

THE SCIENCE OF UNBURDENING EXILES AND HEALING WOUNDS

Exiled parts are wounded, vulnerable and often young. They carry burdens from experiences that terrify, shame or exploit – sometimes all three. With their burdensome feelings and beliefs, they are heavy and threatening to the internal system. But without these burdens they are playful, creative and life-affirming. We believe that exiled parts, like protectors, live in the mind and utilize unintegrated neural networks in the brain. In addition, exiles primarily live within implicit memory (unconscious, tenacious, emotional and without a cohesive narrative). The healing of trauma starts in the mind when we access the imagination, a powerful neuroplastic agent (Doidge, 2007), and continues as we convert implicit to explicit memory so the brain can integrate dysregulated neural networks.

The unburdening process allows exiled parts to let go, release their pain, feel whole again and reintegrate with the inner system of parts. This process seems consistent with memory reconsolidation, a form of neuroplasticity that changes existing emotional memory at the synaptic level (Ecker, 2012). Memory reconsolidation includes four phases: accessing, reactivation, mismatch and erasure.

1) In the accessing phase of memory reconsolidation the client identifies and retrieves implicit emotional memory. In IFS, we do this when we help the client find, focus on and flesh out a target part.

2) In the reactivation phase the emotional memory network is destabilized, which renders it susceptible to being unlocked at the synaptic level. In IFS we are doing this when we help a target part unblend and connect with the client's Self instead of simply reliving its experience.

3) The mismatch phase involves a full disconfirmation of the meaning of the target memory. In IFS we believe the mismatch unfolds as the exiled part feels fully understood, validated and loved by the Self during witnessing, the do-over and retrieval steps, all crucial for healing.

4) In the last phase of erasure the client has the opportunity to revise the meaning of traumatic experience with new learning. Along these lines in IFS, exiles revise their history by letting old meanings go (unburdening toxic sensations, feelings and beliefs) and inviting in new qualities they need. Of course, memory reconsolidation, like IFS therapy, does not cause people to forget the past. It does, however, change their current emotional experiencing when they recall traumatic events.

Counteractive change, the principal strategy of cognitive behavioral therapy (CBT), focuses on creating new networks to compete with old ones while memory reconsolidation on the other hand, reorganizes the original neural network at the synaptic level (Ecker, 2012). We believe the unburdening process in IFS, through the process of memory reconsolidation, heals traumatic wounds at their core.

LEGACY BURDENS

When we speak of "burdens" we mean ongoing negative feeling states (shame, terror, etc.) and beliefs (I'm unlovable, I'm worthless, I'm bad, etc.) that originated in the past. In IFS, legacy burdens are similar but are inherited through family and culture. They can develop in two ways:

- Overtly during interactions with caretakers (often parents or other relatives who may be important in a child's life): an overt legacy burden is created when the caretaker's protector treats the child's parts the way it treats parts of its own internal system (Sinko, 2016).
- Covertly by way of contagion in family and culture: covert legacy burdens are created because children are highly susceptible to the feelings and beliefs of their parents (Sinko, 2016).

THE ORIGINS OF LEGACY BURDENS

A legacy burden often derives from a feeling state that is strongly expressed by a parent or in a family (for example, anxiety), which may or may not come with articulated beliefs (e.g., foreign travel is dangerous) but to which no instructive story is attached. A legacy burden can also derive from the group experience (including the experiences of perpetrators) of one's ancestors, like genocide, slavery, famine or war.

While exiles carry burdens (like "I'm worthless") and tend to be eager for help, and protectors have their own kind of burdens (their jobs are burdensome), which they release along with the exile, a legacy burden is systemic and is held in place either by its invisibility ("it's always been this way") or by loyalty. Legacy burdens, like personal burdens, may derive from mundane misattunements of childhood or from more obviously traumatic events, but they are inherited. Legacy burdens are feelings, beliefs, energy, and behavior whose origins hail from the lives of our ancestors. As a result, legacy burdens can have the generalized, indeterminate quality of family habit and family rules. When the burdening event was seen as shameful and was kept secret at the time, the story is particularly likely to have become "unknown, unrecoverable, vague, or (like the game 'telephone') significantly distorted"(Sinko, 2016, p. 173).

LOYALTY AND LEGACY

Loyalty to caregivers and siblings, family and culture can put a powerful lock on burdens in the client's system, which then governs everything from her choice of partner and work to her health and way of dying (Sinko, 2016).

EPIGENETICS

Recent discoveries in the field of epigenetics also tell us that PTSD is a genetically-inherited disorder, which can be passed down to offspring from either parent (Burri, et al, 2013). IFS has long recognized the intergenerational transmission of trauma in legacy burdens.

HOW LEGACY BURDENS DIFFER FROM PERSONAL BURDENS

Like other burdens, we may hear about a legacy burden at any point. That said, we often discover legacy burdens when protectors are particularly uncooperative and the client's system seems stuck or when a regular unburdening doesn't last. The legacy burden can be carried anywhere in the system, so it may not be carried by an exile. And once the client recognizes that a burden is inherited and not personal, protectors usually want to let it go (Sinko, 2016). If this does not happen and protectors are instead reluctant to let a legacy burden go, we recommend exploring concerns that relate to family loyalty, which is likely to be a factor.

A Legacy Burden

THERAPIST: You keep mentioning that feelings weren't allowed in your family. Are you interested in exploring this more?

NADINE: Sure, it's the way it was – and still is for that matter.

THERAPIST: Go inside and see what comes up for you about feelings not being allowed.

NADINE: I'm seeing my mother telling me not to feel this or that.

> • *A part begins to show its experience to her.*

THERAPIST: Does one particular situation rise to the top?

NADINE: There was a general message from her that feelings are not useful, get in the way and should be pushed away so we can always keep moving forward. That's how it was in my family. As an adult I see how harmful it was.

> • *We call this kind of family culture a legacy burden.*

THERAPIST: It sounds like this was her belief and it influenced you and your brother in negative ways. Is that right?

NADINE: Definitely.

THERAPIST: Do you need this belief?

NADINE: No!

THERAPIST: Would you like to unload it?

NADINE: I didn't realize I could! It's inside me. It's like cellular. I'd love to change that.

THERAPIST: You can release it. I'll show you how.

NADINE: Great! Let's do it.

THERAPIST: Focus on the part or parts who believe that feelings are bad and you shouldn't have them.

NADINE: It's not just one part. It's like … interstitial.

THERAPIST: Does any of it belong to your system?

NADINE: No it belongs to my mother.

THERAPIST: Using your mind's eye, ask your mother if the belief belongs to her.

NADINE: She says it came from her mother.

THERAPIST: Okay. Do they want to share anything with you about this belief?

NADINE: They're both saying it's just the role of women in our family. We are supposed to ignore hardship and keep moving forward.

THERAPIST: Does this make sense to you?

NADINE: Yeah! It's the female cross to bear in my family.

THERAPIST: Well now you have a choice. Knowing it doesn't belong to you, do you want to release it?

NADINE: I am totally ready to unload this. I don't want to live this way for another minute.

THERAPIST: Okay. Find the belief, in or around your body. Got it? What does it look like?

NADINE: It is armor – a metal chest plate. It's medieval actually!

THERAPIST: How do you want to let it go?

NADINE: I'm letting it sink to the bottom of the sea – for crabs and fish to live in.

Nadine's system was willing to let this legacy burden go, which is often—but not always—the case. The best tactic is simply to ask if the client's system is ready to unload a legacy burden. If it is not, then we can spend the time to address fears and uncover the ties that bind.

FIND YOUR
LEGACY BURDENS

DIRECTIONS: Create a family genogram that includes as much as you know (or can find out) about your extended family. There are free online websites that offer a variety of options for types of genograms (for example, http://www.genopro.com/Default-New.aspx).

In your genogram:

- Highlight trauma in general and note specific issues you want to track like alcohol, divorce, domestic violence, incest, multiple childbirths, unsafe living conditions, slavery, racism, substance abuse, war, genocide, starvation, immigration, and the like.

- Also include the positive, such as particular gifts and talents: musical, good at math, mechanical, relationally skilled.

For example:

My maternal grandparents:

- Mary
    - Grew up in New York city, daughter of immigrants from Ireland who worked in factories, alcoholic father, 10 siblings, 2 died in infancy.

- Colin
    - Grew up in upstate New York, the son of a plumber and a housewife who had a "nervous breakdown" when Colin was 10 years old.

- Their children
    - My mother, Sybil
    - Aunt Eleanor
    - Uncle Edward (died accidentally at 15 years old)

My parents:

- Sybil: school teacher
- Joseph: accountant
    - My siblings and me
        ◊ Me
        ◊ Liam: housepainter, alcohol problem, 1 child
        ◊ Marie: nurse, 2 children

Aunt Eleanor: gave up ambition to be an opera singer

- Her husband Al: car mechanic
    - My cousins
        ◊ Sharon: talented singer, no children
        ◊ Dale: works as an actuary, 3 children

Notice repeating patterns of strength and vulnerability in the ancestral map and write them down below, use extra paper as needed.

Strengths:

_____

_____

_____

_____

Vulnerabilities:

_____

_____

_____

_____

Choose an ancestral vulnerability that also resides in you and has influenced your life.

- Turn your attention inside and ask permission to pay attention to this vulnerability.
- If there are concerns, listen to them and either set an intention to return to this with the help of a therapist or, if you get permission, proceed.
- Notice the vulnerability in, on or around your body.
- Ask the following question and write down what you hear without censoring or thinking:
  - What percentage of this vulnerability belongs to me, and what percentage belongs to my parents (or someone else from your early life)?

_____% belongs to me.

_____% belongs to _____.

SECTION
6

Treatment Tips

OPTIONS FOR ENDING A SESSION

Some people close their eyes for much or all of a session and are likely to lose track of time; others do not. Some people like a 5-minute warning; others may prefer a longer lead-time. Depending on a client's preference, you can say something like this to wrap up a session:

- "We have just a few minutes left today…."
- "We are almost out of time…."
- "We'll need to finish soon…."

Then, depending on what's happening, offer some options:

- If you are negotiating with a protector:
    - "We have to stop in a couple of minutes, would this part like us to come back next week and pay attention?"
- If the answer is no:
    - "Okay. Would it be okay to return next week just to keep talking about this?"
- If witnessing an exile:
    - "Where would this part like to be between now and our next session that would feel safe and comfortable?"

BETWEEN SESSIONS FOR CLIENTS

If you are in dialogue with a part, you will want to set an intention to return.

- "Where would this part like to be in the meantime? It doesn't have to move, but if it would like to stay somewhere else it can be in any time or any place. Ask it to show you where it would like to be and what it will need there during the week."
- "If the part would like this, would you be available to check in?"
- If yes:
    - "If you say you'll do this, be sure to follow through. Is there a time of day that you could check in regularly, like when you wake up or go to bed?"

Sometimes parts just want to be able to call on the client if needed, in which case ask:

- "How would this part like to get your attention if it wants you? And what will you say to it if you can't pay attention in that exact moment?"

- If the client says "I don't know" offer options:
  - "You could say 'I'm busy right now but I will get back to you at 4 pm when I'm done with these phone calls,' or whatever the situation requires. But if you set that intention, write yourself a note so that you do it. To be trusted, be consistent."

After closing with the target part, check with the system as a whole.

- "Does any part want you to know anything or want anything from you before we stop today?"
- "Does anyone want anything from you during the coming week?"
- "Okay, let's have all your parts go back inside and take back their energy so you can function in your life between now and our next session."

BETWEEN SESSIONS FOR THERAPISTS

It is a good practice for therapist's to take a few minutes in between sessions to check-in with their parts. Parts can get activated by the previous client and need some attention, or other parts might be nervous and apprehensive about the upcoming client.

You can make a regular practice of using the following meditation between sessions to clear the energy of your activated parts so that you are open and available with your next client.

Meditation

THERAPIST CHECK-IN
BETWEEN SESSIONS

- Close your eyes (if that feels comfortable) and ask inside if your previous client triggered any of your parts.

- Ask your parts if they need anything from you now. See if they are willing to relax.
    - If not, set an intention with them to follow-up at a later time – and be specific about when you will check back with them – and then ask them to go into a waiting room (in your mind) while you see your next client.

- Make room inside to bring Self-energy to the experience of being triggered by your last client.

- When those parts step back, notice the internal space that is created.

- Now ask if your parts feel apprehensive about your next client.
    - Listen to their concerns and let them know that they can rest near you during the session or, if it would feel more comfortable, they can go into a waiting room.
    - Ask if they can trust your Self to handle the next session.

- Again, connect with your Self before you proceed with your next client.

TROUBLE-SHOOTING: COMMON OBSTACLES AND FAQ'S

- The client doesn't like the IFS language and is puzzled by the idea of parts.
  - Knowing the client is talking about a part, stay with the client's language. "So when you get angry," or "When you eat too much."
- The client is uncomfortable paying attention to internal experiencing: sensations, feelings or thoughts.
  - Ask for permission to find out why and then listen to the reasons. Often the problem is exile overwhelm or fear of giving an extreme protector too much power.
- The client believes parts are evidence of pathology.
  - We normalize psychic multiplicity and validate the positive intention of parts.
- The client is compliant but not engaged.
  - Make this observation in a friendly way and ask if it's okay to be curious about it. Then find the part (usually a Self-like part) who is taking the client out and ask about its motive.
- The client's parts present in a confusing whirl.
  - Be patient, observe that this is the case, inquire why such a presentation might be important.
- The client just wants to tell stories and ask your opinion.
  - Appreciate this protector and ask if it is willing to be direct about its concerns instead of blocking other parts from having a chance to be heard.
- The client is blended with a difficult or scary part:
  - An exile with intense negative feelings that threaten to overwhelm.
  - A cruel critic.
  - A self-harming or suicidal part.
  - An enraged part.
  - Use direct access to talk to the part.
- The client's protectors won't make room for the Self.
  - Trust your Self to take the lead and explore.
  - There may be an activated Self-like part.
  - A protective part may have negative feelings toward the client's Self.

Other Applications of IFS Therapy

COMMON CONCERNS ABOUT PRACTICING IFS

1) I don't have enough experience or training as an IFS therapist.

    a. Inexperienced IFS therapists can talk to protectors safely but should not attempt to work with exiles.

2) I don't feel confident about managing the difficulties that will arise.

    a. Confidence comes with experience. Therapists who have little experience or training in IFS can still interview protectors safely.

    b. We also recommend formal training and supervision from an experienced IFS therapist as well as direct experience in IFS therapy.

COMMON QUESTIONS ABOUT PRACTICING IFS

1) Can I integrate IFS with my previous training?

    a. As long as you can be curious, validating, compassionate and polite with the client's parts (that is, be Self-led), feel free to try integrating the skills you know and trust.

    b. Be aware that IFS does differ from more traditional approaches to trauma therapy in some important ways (Anderson & Sweezy, 2016).

    c. We recommend doing therapy with an overall IFS framework and integrate other modalities in as you see fit. For example, do a piece of CBT, EMDR or body work with a specific protective part, if it is willing.

2) What should I do if an exile is unintentionally triggered?

    a. Apologize to the client's protectors, let them know this was not your goal and validate their need to do their jobs.

Many seasoned, talented IFS trained therapists are adapting IFS to different therapy populations and therapy modalities in the United States and elsewhere. The list below is not all-inclusive. For more publications and information, please go to The Center for Self-leadership website: https://www.selfleadership.org.

THERAPY MODALITIES

Couples

In her adaptation of IFS to couple therapy (Intimacy from the Inside Out or IFIO) Toni Herbine-Blank emphasizes the importance of good communication for intimate relationships. By teaching partners to speak for parts and from the Self, IFIO helps them be with their differences, forego internal as well as external shaming and stay with hard conversations until each feels fully heard, understood and able to live with differences (Herbine-Blank, 2013; Herbine-Blank, Kerpelman & Sweezy, 2016).

Toni Herbine-Blank, MSN: Senior IFS trainer + Training Developer and Director of Intimacy from the Inside Out, www.toniherbineblank.com

Stepfamilies

In her work with stepfamilies, Patricia Papernow uses IFS to illuminate five major challenges created by stepfamily structure. For each challenge, three levels of clinical work help extreme parts relax and support the Self-leadership required to meet these challenges: I. *Psychoeducational*: Providing information about how stepfamilies are different from first-time families, what works, and what doesn't to meet the challenges. II. *Interpersonal*: Supporting Self-to-Self connection in the face of the divisive forces of stepfamily structure. III. *Intrapsychic*: When reactivity remains high (or low), using IFS to heal old family-of-origin bruises that may be driving reactivity (Papernow, 2013).

Patricia Papernow: *Surviving and Thriving in Stepfamily Relationships: What Works and What Doesn't,* www.stepfamilyrelationships.com, ppapernow@gmail.com

Children and Adolescents

In her adaptation of IFS for children and adolescents, Pamela Krause points out that kids, who are powerless relative to adults, must influence family dynamics and adult behavior indirectly. Symptoms, which symbolize that indirection, lead us to the parts who problem-solve internally. Krause illustrates how we can use IFS to help parents unblend from their protectors while children externalize and get into relationship with their parts, so they can validate the concerns of protectors and heal their exiled wounds. (Krause, 2013).

Pamela Krause: pamela.krause@gmail.com, 717-732-6055

Parenting Adult Children

In his adaptation of IFS to the challenges of parenting adult children, Paul Neustadt differentiates Self-led parenting from reactive parenting. The Self-led parent can see the present with perspective and clarity while the parent who is blended with protectors reacts to the present situation as if it is a negative experience from the past. Neustadt illustrates how the IFS approach can help parents unblend from protectors and parent from the Self (Neustadt, 2016).

Paul Neustadt: probneus@gmail.com

Groups

Group therapy is an umbrella term that covers a wide variety of options for a variety of very different populations. Although as yet there are no publications that describe how to use IFS in group therapy, many skilled practitioners are using IFS with groups. Our observation is that the basic principles of IFS (everyone has parts and when protective parts differentiate the Self is there to heal injured parts) can be adapted to group therapy for many client populations, including trauma survivors, depression, anxiety, eating disorders and addiction.

Movement

In her somatically-based adaptation of IFS, Susan McConnell locates the physical manifestations of attachment injuries and trauma and illustrates how the IFS therapist can use breath, movement and touch to embody the Self, be in relationship with parts and from this vantage witness, unburden and integrate these parts back into the internal system (McConnell, 2013).

Susan McConnell: susanmccon@gmail.com, embodiedself.net

TRAUMA

Post-Traumatic Stress Disorder (PTSD), Dissociative Identity Disorder (DID), Disorders of Extreme Stress Not Otherwise Specified (DESNOS)

In their application of IFS with trauma, Frank Anderson and Martha Sweezy differentiate IFS from standard trauma treatment: Standard treatment divides therapy into phases and offers various practices that are intended to help the client stabilize before moving on to some variety of exposure-based options for processing traumatic memories. In contrast, IFS welcomes extreme symptoms or parts at the onset, developing (inside and out) a way of relating that culminates in love and has the relational power to disconfirm the various assaultive falsehoods that trauma promotes (*I am unlovable, I am worthless*) (Anderson & Sweezy, 2016).

Frank Anderson: FrankAndersonMD.com, Frank@FrankAndersonMD.com

Martha Sweezy, Northampton, MA, 617-669-7656, http://marthasweezy.com

The Trauma of Chronic Physical illness and Physical Illness Related to Trauma

In her adaptation of IFS to chronic illness, Nancy Sowell illustrates the ways in which soothing and healing the heart with the practice of profound self-acceptance in IFS eases the emotional and physiological dysregulation that typically follows trauma. Additionally, the conflicts that often accompany chronic illness, such as stoicism vs. fear and sadness, soften. This softening leads to improved self-compassion, empowerment and healing for body as well as heart (Sowell, 2013).

Nancy Sowell: www.nancysowell.com

MENTAL ILLNESSES THAT ARE TRAUMATIC

Bipolar Disorder and Schizophrenia

No study has been done to date and we don't know of any publications on the topic of IFS being used to treat major mental illness. We do know from clinical experience that major mental illness is in itself traumatic and we look forward to exploring the use of IFS with clients who are having these experiences.

MENTAL ILLNESSES THAT MAY RELATE TO TRAUMA AS WELL AS BIOLOGY

Depression and Anxiety

In the process of exploring the particular strengths of IFS, Martha Sweezy speculates that IFS is effective with a broad swath of psychic suffering because self-compassion, which is the centerpiece of IFS, is mutually exclusive with self-shaming, and shame has a seminal role in a wide variety of symptoms, including depression and anxiety (Sweezy, 2016).

Martha Sweezy, Northampton, MA, 617-669-7656, http://marthasweezy.com

SEXUALITY

Welcoming All Sexual Parts and Reactions to the Erotic

Employing the concepts of IFS in relation to sexuality, Larry Rosenberg points out that parts internalize polarized cultural messages about sexuality – ranging from excited desire to shameful inhibition – and he posits that the erotic consists of essential yin-yang polarizations, with erotic stimulation benefiting from the opportunity to play with conflicting tensions. When therapists unburden their anxious or judging parts they can help clients explore their sexual functioning, identities, desires and behaviors (Rosenberg, 2013).

Larry Rosenberg, Ph.D., 1105 Massachusetts Ave. Suite 3F, Cambridge, MA 02138, 617-491-1085, larry_rosenberg@hms.harvard.edu

LOSS

Self-led Grieving

In his adaptation of IFS to grief therapy, Derek Scott differentiates between simple and complicated grief. The former is straightforward and requires the IFS therapist to embody Self-energy while being a companion and guide (as needed) for the bereaved client. The latter, complicated grief, leads to parts who have experienced unsupported loss in the past and who need the love and compassion of the client's Self in order to heal (Scott, 2016).

Derek Scott: 519-438-6777, derek@derekscott.com, www.derekscott.com

OPPRESSION

Racism (and all forms of othering or bigotry, including homophobia, transphobia, misogyny, xenophobia)

To address his own racism, Richard Schwartz befriended his racist parts and learned about their protective roles. He points out that the challenge of acknowledging our bigotry, especially our hidden bigotry, is less of a minefield when we think and speak in terms of parts – and the Self – because the racist beliefs and behavior of some of our parts does not define us globally. In addition, he illustrates how helping all our parts feel securely attached and safe internally frees aggressive protectors from their onerous (mostly disowned) jobs. By facilitating Self-led conversations, Schwartz has been able to mobilize people – even people who are at war (specifically, the Israelis and the Palestinians) – to address the injuries of racism at both a personal and a communal level (Schwartz, 2016).

Richard Schwartz: https://www.selfleadership.org

EXTREME PROTECTION

Perpetrator Parts

Using IFS in therapy with perpetrators, Richard Schwartz learned that perpetrator parts are a distinct class of protector: they have a drive to dominate and humiliate, they experience relief when they are in a position of power, they despise and make a point of punishing vulnerability internally and in others, and they show no concern for consequences or the feelings of those whom they victimize. Although these parts are destructive and scary, Schwartz points out that they were not born to behave this way or do this job. In fact, protectors don't like doing their jobs and they do change once the parts they protect are healed (Schwartz, 2016).

Richard Schwartz: https://www.selfleadership.org

THE COSTLY DISTRACTION OF ADDICTIONS

Alcohol and Drugs

In her adaptation of IFS to addiction treatment, Cece Sykes helps clients see the typical addict polarity between harsh self-management and compulsive risk-taking and how protectors caught in both roles have positive intentions. Her overarching goal is help clients achieve the self-compassion they need to restore inner balance and heal (Sykes, 2016).

Cece Sykes, LCSW, 708-903-4348, www.cecesykeslcsw.com, cecesykes427@gmail.com

Pornography

Avoiding the standard shaming approach of treatment for sex addicts, Nancy Wonder's first aim as she applies IFS with pornography addicts is for the therapist to be Self-led while exploring the inner polarity that grips the client: a part who loves porn and another part who views the client as weak, embarrassing and despicable for needing porn to distract and self-soothe. Welcoming the protectors on both sides of this polarity helps the client become Self-led, heal exiled parts and let go of the compulsive illusion of comfort (Wonder, 2013).

Nancy Wonder specializes in attachment wounding, sexual abuse, and sexual acting-out: 850-222-7112, nancywonder@icloud.com

Eating Disorders

Anorexia, Bulimia, Binge-eating

Describing the use of IFS with eating disorders, Jeanne Catanzaro explains that the ED client has polarized protectors who are afraid of each other and of the exiled feelings that arise when they relax. Using IFS, the therapist can validate the fears of these well-intended parts and deescalate their conflict in order to access and heal the underlying injury (Catanzaro, 2016).

Jeanne Catanzaro: jeannecatanzarophd@gmail.com

BEYOND PSYCHOTHERAPY

Psychopharmacology

In his adaptation of IFS to psychopharmacology, Frank Anderson articulates five strategies for prescribing. First he identifies a list of symptoms and opens a dialogue with parts so he can differentiate a biological condition from the behavior of a part. Next he validates parts' previous experiences with medication and addresses their concerns about the future. After this, he prescribes only if all parts are in agreement. Once consensus is reached, he educates parts about what to expect from medications and invites them to stay in communication about their experience. Last, he helps his own parts to unblend so that he can be Self-led in the role of educator while the client makes the decisions (Anderson, 2013).

Frank Anderson: FrankAndersonMD.com, Frank@FrankAndersonMD.com

Mindfulness

In his introduction to *Internal Family Systems Therapy: New Dimensions* Jack Engler writes about his personal therapy experiences with IFS and some notable parallels and differences between Schwartz's concept of "Self" and the teachings of various spiritual traditions. While most spiritual practices seek to access that which is already whole, aware and awake in us, Engler notes that there are a couple of key differences between the IFS approach and most spiritual traditions: first, the Self is interactive and, second, accessing the Self does not require years of disciplined practice (Engler, 2013).

Jack Engler, Ph.D.: 266 Peakham Road, Sudbury, MA 01776, 978-460-4259, jackengler@verizon.net

Health coaching

In their adaptation of IFS to health coaching (Self-aware informational nonjudgmental health coaching or SINHC™), John Livingstone and Joanne Gaffney teach health coaches to be aware of the feelings and beliefs of their own parts so they can be emotionally available to the patient. Using direct access with the patient's parts (called "information interweave™") SINHC trained coaches do not offer advice at the outset of contact. Instead, they listen for the feelings and beliefs of the patient's parts. By expressing interest and validating concerns, the coach helps protective parts relax so the patient can hear evidence-based information and make Self-led decisions. (Livingstone & Gaffney, 2013) Joanne Gaffney: 508 487-0400, jgaffneyliving@gmail.com

John B. Livingstone: Health, Athletic, and Executive Coaching Science, Gaffney & Livingstone Consultants, 522 Commercial St, Provincetown, MA 02657, jlivingstoneservices@comcast.net, 508-487-0455, 617-413-7131

Creativity

In her introduction to *Innovations and Elaborations in Internal Family Systems Therapy*, Janna Malamud Smith compares the IFS psychotherapy process, in which psychic processes are concretized as clients and parts interact, with the way fiction, poetry and drama tap into the same essential process of mind as writers locate and inhabit different perspectives – not only of their characters but of their characters' parts (Smith, 2016).

Janna Smith is a regular contributor to WBUR's Cognoscenti: Jannamalamudsmith.com, jannamsmith@verizon.net

Research Related to IFS

Michael Mithoefer and his research group have been studying the effects of the drug 3,4-methylenedioxymethamphetamine (MDMA – recreational name Ecstasy) to assist in psychotherapy with war veterans, firefighters, police officers, and individuals who have PTSD due to rape, assault or childhood abuse. Mithoefer, a psychiatrist who is trained in IFS, wrote: "MDMA fosters a pronounced increase in Self energy in clients who take the drug, along with an increased awareness of their parts and the ability to differentiate from them." His results, both short and long term, have been remarkable for the reduction of PTSD symptoms.

Michael Mithoefer: mmithoefer@mac.com

A study published in the *Journal of Rheumatology* in 2013 (Shadick, et al) showed that IFS treatment has favorable effects on patients with rheumatoid arthritis. This study was submitted to NREPP (the National Registry for Evidence-based Programs and Practices), which resulted in their endorsement of IFS as an *evidence-based practice*. In particular, they found promising effects of IFS on the mind (depression, anxiety), the body (physical health conditions), and the spirit (personal resilience and self-concept).

Recently, the Foundation for Self Leadership, a non-profit organization dedicated to the advancement of IFS through research, scholarship and advocacy beyond psychotherapy, has supported two pilot studies entitled: *IFS Therapy for the Treatment of PTSD and Complex Trauma* and *Exploring the Phenomenology, Physiology, and Dyadic Processes of an IFS Intervention*. The latter study hypothesizes that IFS has physiological effects on the therapist, the client, and the therapeutic relationship between them. Meanwhile, results from the PTSD and Complex Trauma study demonstrate significant reductions in symptoms of PTSD and depression in 12 of the 13 subjects after completing 16 weeks of IFS treatment. If you are interested in learning more about IFS research please visit the Foundation for Self Leadership online. FoundationIFS.org

References

American Psychiatric Association. (2013). *Diagnostic and statistical manual of mental disorders* (5th ed.). Arlington, VA: American Psychiatric Publishing.

Anderson, F. G. (2013). "Who's Taking What?" Connecting Neuroscience, Psychopharmacology and Internal Family Systems for Trauma. In: M. Sweezy & E. L. Ziskind (Eds.), *Internal family systems therapy: New dimensions* (p. 107-126). Oxford, U.K.: Routledge.

Anderson, F. G., Sweezy M. (2016). What IFS Offers to the Treatment of Trauma. In: M. Sweezy & E. L. Ziskind (Eds.), *Innovations and elaborations in internal family systems therapy* (p. 133-147). Oxford, U.K.: Routledge.

Anderson, F. G., (2016). Here's How Neuroscience Can Shift Your Client's Emotions in an Instant. *Psychotherapy Networker*. Nov./Dec. 2016.

Burri, A., Küffer, A., Maercker, A. (2013, January 16). Epigenetic Mechanisms in Post-Traumatic Stress Disorder. *StressPoints*. Retrieved from http://www.istss.org/education-research/traumatic-stresspoints/2013-january/epigenetic-mechanisms-in-post-traumatic-stress-dis.aspx

Catanzaro, J. (2016). IFS and Eating Disorders: Healing the Parts Who Hide in Plain Sight. In: M. Sweezy & E. L. Ziskind (Eds.), *Innovations and elaborations in internal family systems therapy* (p. 49-69). Oxford, U.K.: Routledge.

D'Andrea, W., Ford, J., Stolbach, B., Spinazzola, J., van der Kolk, B. A. (2012). Understanding Interpersonal Trauma in Children: Why We Need a Developmentally Appropriate Trauma Diagnosis, *American Journal of Orthopsychiatry 82*, 187-200.

Ecker, B., Ticic, R., Hulley, L. (2012). *Unlocking the emotional brain: Eliminating symptoms at their roots using memory reconsolidation.* London, U.K.: Routledge.

Engler, J. (2013). An Introduction to IFS. In: M. Sweezy & E. L. Ziskind (Eds.), *Internal family systems therapy: New dimensions* (p. xvii-xxvii). Oxford, U.K.: Routledge.

Fisher, S. F. (2014). *Neurofeedback in the treatment of developmental trauma: Calming the fear-driven brain.* New York, NY: W. W. Norton & Company, Inc.

Geib, P. (2016). Expanded Unburdenings: Relaxing Managers and Releasing Creativity. In: M. Sweezy & E. L. Ziskind (Eds.), *Innovations and elaborations in internal family systems therapy* (p. 148-163). Oxford, U.K.: Routledge.

Herbine-Blank, T. (2016). Self in Relationship: An Introduction to IFS Couple Therapy. In: M. Sweezy & E. L. Ziskind (Eds.), *Internal family systems therapy: New dimensions* (p. 55-71). Oxford, U.K.: Routledge.

Herbine-Blank T, Kerpelman D, Sweezy, M. (2015). *Intimacy from the inside out: Courage and compassion in couple therapy.* Oxford, U.K.: Routledge.

Herman, J. L., Perry, C. J., Van der Kolk, B. A. (1989, April). Childhood trauma in borderline personality disorder. *American Journal of Psychiatry, 146*(4), 490-495 (ISSN: 0002-953X).

Herman, J. L. (1992). *Trauma and recovery.* United States: Basic Books.

International Society for the Study of Trauma and Dissociation (2011). Guidelines for treating dissociative identity disorder in adults, third revision: Summary version. *Journal of Trauma & Dissociation, 12*, 188–212.

Kabat-Zinn, J. (2003, June). Mindfulness-Based Interventions in Context: Past, Present, and Future. *Clinical Psychology: Science and Practice 10*(2), 144–156.

Kagan, J. (2010). *The temperamental thread: How genes, culture, time and luck make us who we are.* New York: the Dana Foundation.

Krause, P. IFS with Children and Adolescents (2013). In: M. Sweezy & E. L. Ziskind (Eds.), *Internal family systems therapy: New dimensions* (p. 35-54). Oxford, U.K.: Routledge.

Krause P., Rosenberg L.G., Sweezy M. (2016). Getting Unstuck. In: Sweezy M., Ziskind E. L. (Eds.), *Innovations and elaborations in internal family systems therapy* (p. 10-28). Oxford, U.K.: Routledge.

Lanius R. A., Bluhm R. L., Coupland N. J., Hegadoren K. M., Rowe B., Théberge J., Neufeld R. W., Williamson P. C., Brimson M. (2010, January). Default mode network connectivity as a predictor of post-traumatic stress disorder symptom severity in acutely traumatized subjects. *Acta Psychiatrica Scandinavica.*121(1):33-40.

Linehan, M. (1993). *Cognitive-behavioral treatment of borderline personality disorder.* New York: Guilford.

Livingstone, J. B., Gaffney, J. (2013). IFS and Health Coaching: A New Model of Behavior Change and Medical Decision Making. In: M. Sweezy & E. L. Ziskind (Eds.), *Internal family systems therapy: New dimensions* (p. 143-158). Oxford, U.K.: Routledge.

McConnell, S. (2013). Embodying the Internal Family. In: M. Sweezy & E. L. Ziskind (Eds.), *Internal family systems therapy: New dimensions* (p. 90-106). Oxford, U.K.: Routledge.

Neustadt, P. (2016). From Reactive to Self-Led Parenting: IFS Therapy for Parents. In: M. Sweezy & E. L. Ziskind (Eds.), *Innovations and elaborations in internal family systems therapy* (p. 70-89). Oxford, U.K.: Routledge.

Northoff G., Bermpohl F., (2004, March). Cortical Midline Structures and the Self. *Trends in Cognitive Science. 8*(3), 102-7.

Papernow, P (2013). *Surviving and thriving in stepfamily relationships: What works and what doesn't.* New York, NY: Routledge.

Porges, S (2011). *The polyvagal theory: Neurophysiological foundations of emotions, attachment, communication, and self-regulation.* New York: W.W. Norton.

Rosenberg, L. G. (2013). Welcoming All Erotic Parts: Our Reaction to the Sexual and Using Polarities to Enhance Erotic Excitement. In: M. Sweezy & E. L. Ziskind (Eds.), *Internal family systems therapy: New dimensions* (p. 166-185). Oxford, U.K.: Routledge.

Schwartz R. C. (2013). The Therapist Client Relationship and the Transformative Power of Self. In: M. Sweezy & E. L. Ziskind (Eds.), *Internal family systems therapy: New dimensions* (p. 1-23). Oxford, U.K.: Routledge.

Schwartz R. C. (2016). Perpetrator Parts. In: M. Sweezy & E. L. Ziskind (Eds.), *Innovations and elaborations in internal family systems therapy* (p. 109-122). Oxford, U.K.: Routledge.

Schwartz, R. C. (2016). Dealing With Racism: Should We Exorcise or Embrace Our Inner Bigots? In: M. Sweezy & E. L. Ziskind (Eds.), *Innovations and elaborations in internal family systems therapy* (p. 124-132). Oxford, U.K.: Routledge.

Scott, D. (2016). Self-Led Grieving: Transitions, Loss and Death. In: M. Sweezy & E. L. Ziskind (Eds.), *Innovations and elaborations in internal family systems therapy* (p. 90-108). Oxford, U.K.: Routledge.

Seppala, E. (2012). The Brain's Ability to Look Within: A Secret to Well-Being. *The Creativity Post*, Dec. 30. Retrieved from http://www.creativitypost.com/psychology/the_brains_ability_to_look_within_a_secret_to_well_being

Siegel, D. J. (2017). *Mind: A journey to the heart of being human*. New York, NY: Norton.

Singer, T, Klimecki O. (2014, September). Empathy and Compassion. *Current Biology, 24*(18), R875-R878.

Sinko, A. L. (2016). Legacy Burdens. In: M. Sweezy & E.L. Ziskind (Eds.), *Innovations and elaborations in internal family systems therapy* (p. 164-178). Oxford, U.K.: Routledge.

Smith J. M. (2016). Introduction. In: M. Sweezy & E. L. Ziskind (Eds.), *Innovations and elaborations in internal family systems therapy* (p. 1-9). Oxford, U.K.: Routledge.

Sowell, N. (2013). The Internal Family System and Adult Health: Changing the Course of Chronic Illness. In: M. Sweezy & E. L. Ziskind (Eds.), *Internal family systems therapy: New dimensions* (p. 127-142). Oxford, U.K.: Routledge.

Sweezy M. (2013). Emotional Cannibalism: Shame in Action. In: M. Sweezy & E. L. Ziskind (Eds.), *Internal family systems therapy: New dimensions* (p. 24-34). Oxford, U.K.: Routledge.

Sykes C. (2016). An IFS Lens on Addiction: Compassion for Extreme Parts. In: M. Sweezy & E. L. Ziskind (Eds.), *Innovations and elaborations in internal family systems therapy* (p. 29-48). Oxford, U.K.: Routledge.

Van der Kolk, B. A. (2014). *The body keeps the score: Brain, mind and body in the healing of trauma*. New York, NY: Viking Press.

Van der Kolk, B. A. (2005). Developmental Trauma Disorder: Toward a Rational Diagnosis for Children with Complex Trauma Histories, *Psychiatric Annals 35*(5), 401-8.

Wonder, N. (2013). Treating Pornography Addiction with IFS. In: M. Sweezy & E. L. Ziskind (Eds.), *Internal family systems therapy: New dimensions* (p. 159-165). Oxford, U.K.: Routledge.

Printed in Great Britain
by Amazon